50 Perfect Pizza Recipes for Home

By: Kelly Johnson

Table of Contents

- Margherita Pizza
- Pepperoni Pizza
- Hawaiian Pizza
- BBQ Chicken Pizza
- Supreme Pizza
- Veggie Lover's Pizza
- Meat Lover's Pizza
- Buffalo Chicken Pizza
- White Pizza
- Pesto Chicken Pizza
- Mediterranean Pizza
- Caprese Pizza
- Four Cheese Pizza
- Sausage and Mushroom Pizza
- Spinach and Feta Pizza
- Taco Pizza
- Philly Cheesesteak Pizza
- Breakfast Pizza
- Chicken Alfredo Pizza
- Shrimp Scampi Pizza
- Artichoke and Spinach Pizza
- Prosciutto and Arugula Pizza
- Truffle Oil Pizza
- Bacon and Egg Pizza
- Cauliflower Crust Pizza
- Gluten-Free Pizza
- Deep Dish Pizza
- Thin Crust Pizza
- Stuffed Crust Pizza
- Sicilian Pizza
- Neapolitan Pizza
- Chicago-style Deep Dish Pizza
- Detroit-style Pizza
- Calzone
- Stromboli
- BBQ Pulled Pork Pizza

- Thai Chicken Pizza
- Teriyaki Chicken Pizza
- Fig and Goat Cheese Pizza
- Mushroom and Gorgonzola Pizza
- Margherita with Burrata Pizza
- Caramelized Onion and Brie Pizza
- Pear and Gorgonzola Pizza
- Chicken Tikka Masala Pizza
- Tandoori Paneer Pizza
- Mediterranean Lamb Pizza
- Brussels Sprouts and Bacon Pizza
- Peking Duck Pizza
- Ratatouille Pizza
- Blueberry Dessert Pizza

Margherita Pizza

Ingredients:

Pizza Dough:

- 1⅓ cups warm water (about 105°F or 40°C)
- 2¼ teaspoons active dry yeast (1 packet)
- 3½ cups all-purpose flour
- 2 tablespoons olive oil
- 1½ teaspoons salt
- 1 teaspoon sugar

Pizza Toppings:

- 1 can (14-ounce) crushed tomatoes (preferably San Marzano)
- 2 cloves garlic, minced
- Salt and pepper to taste
- 8 ounces fresh mozzarella cheese, sliced
- Fresh basil leaves
- Extra-virgin olive oil, for drizzling

Instructions:

1. Prepare the Dough:

- In a small bowl, combine warm water, yeast, and sugar. Let it sit for 5-10 minutes until foamy.
- In a large mixing bowl, combine flour and salt. Make a well in the center and add the yeast mixture and olive oil.
- Stir until a dough forms, then knead on a floured surface for about 5-7 minutes until smooth and elastic.
- Place dough in an oiled bowl, cover with a damp cloth, and let it rise in a warm place for about 1-2 hours until doubled in size.

2. Prepare the Sauce:

- In a small saucepan, heat a tablespoon of olive oil over medium heat. Add minced garlic and cook for about 1 minute until fragrant.
- Add crushed tomatoes, salt, and pepper. Simmer for 15-20 minutes until the sauce thickens slightly. Remove from heat and let it cool.

3. Preheat and Prepare Pizza:

- Preheat your oven to its highest temperature (usually around 500°F or 260°C) and place a pizza stone or inverted baking sheet inside to heat.

- Punch down the dough and divide it into two equal portions. On a floured surface, stretch or roll out each portion into a circle (about 10-12 inches in diameter).

4. Assemble the Pizza:

- Place the stretched dough onto a piece of parchment paper.
- Spread half of the tomato sauce evenly over the dough, leaving a small border around the edges.
- Arrange half of the sliced mozzarella evenly over the sauce.

5. Bake the Pizza:

- Using a pizza peel or inverted baking sheet, carefully transfer the pizza (with the parchment paper) onto the preheated pizza stone or baking sheet in the oven.
- Bake for 10-12 minutes, or until the crust is golden and the cheese is bubbly and slightly browned.

6. Finish and Serve:

- Remove the pizza from the oven and let it cool for a minute. Sprinkle fresh basil leaves over the top and drizzle with extra-virgin olive oil.
- Slice and serve hot.

Enjoy your homemade Margherita pizza!

Pepperoni Pizza

Ingredients:

Pizza Dough:

- 1⅓ cups warm water (about 105°F or 40°C)
- 2¼ teaspoons active dry yeast (1 packet)
- 3½ cups all-purpose flour
- 2 tablespoons olive oil
- 1½ teaspoons salt
- 1 teaspoon sugar

Pizza Toppings:

- 1 can (14-ounce) crushed tomatoes (preferably San Marzano)
- 2 cloves garlic, minced
- Salt and pepper to taste
- 8 ounces mozzarella cheese, shredded or sliced
- 3 ounces pepperoni slices (about 30 slices)
- Fresh basil leaves (optional)
- Grated Parmesan cheese (optional)
- Red pepper flakes (optional)

Instructions:

1. Prepare the Dough:

- In a small bowl, combine warm water, yeast, and sugar. Let it sit for 5-10 minutes until foamy.
- In a large mixing bowl, combine flour and salt. Make a well in the center and add the yeast mixture and olive oil.
- Stir until a dough forms, then knead on a floured surface for about 5-7 minutes until smooth and elastic.
- Place dough in an oiled bowl, cover with a damp cloth, and let it rise in a warm place for about 1-2 hours until doubled in size.

2. Prepare the Sauce:

- In a small saucepan, heat a tablespoon of olive oil over medium heat. Add minced garlic and cook for about 1 minute until fragrant.
- Add crushed tomatoes, salt, and pepper. Simmer for 15-20 minutes until the sauce thickens slightly. Remove from heat and let it cool.

3. Preheat and Prepare Pizza:

- Preheat your oven to its highest temperature (usually around 500°F or 260°C) and place a pizza stone or inverted baking sheet inside to heat.
- Punch down the dough and divide it into two equal portions. On a floured surface, stretch or roll out each portion into a circle (about 10-12 inches in diameter).

4. Assemble the Pizza:

- Place the stretched dough onto a piece of parchment paper.
- Spread half of the tomato sauce evenly over the dough, leaving a small border around the edges.
- Sprinkle half of the shredded mozzarella cheese evenly over the sauce.
- Arrange the pepperoni slices over the cheese.

5. Bake the Pizza:

- Using a pizza peel or inverted baking sheet, carefully transfer the pizza (with the parchment paper) onto the preheated pizza stone or baking sheet in the oven.
- Bake for 10-12 minutes, or until the crust is golden and the cheese is bubbly and slightly browned.

6. Finish and Serve:

- Remove the pizza from the oven and let it cool for a minute. Optionally, sprinkle with fresh basil leaves, grated Parmesan cheese, and red pepper flakes for extra flavor.
- Slice and serve hot.

Enjoy your delicious homemade Pepperoni Pizza!

Hawaiian Pizza

Ingredients:

Pizza Dough:

- 1⅓ cups warm water (about 105°F or 40°C)
- 2¼ teaspoons active dry yeast (1 packet)
- 3½ cups all-purpose flour
- 2 tablespoons olive oil
- 1½ teaspoons salt
- 1 teaspoon sugar

Pizza Toppings:

- 1 can (14-ounce) crushed tomatoes (preferably San Marzano)
- 2 cloves garlic, minced
- Salt and pepper to taste
- 8 ounces mozzarella cheese, shredded or sliced
- 6-8 slices of ham, chopped or torn into pieces
- 1 cup pineapple chunks (fresh or canned, drained)
- Fresh basil leaves (optional)
- Red pepper flakes (optional)

Instructions:

1. Prepare the Dough:

- In a small bowl, combine warm water, yeast, and sugar. Let it sit for 5-10 minutes until foamy.
- In a large mixing bowl, combine flour and salt. Make a well in the center and add the yeast mixture and olive oil.
- Stir until a dough forms, then knead on a floured surface for about 5-7 minutes until smooth and elastic.
- Place dough in an oiled bowl, cover with a damp cloth, and let it rise in a warm place for about 1-2 hours until doubled in size.

2. Prepare the Sauce:

- In a small saucepan, heat a tablespoon of olive oil over medium heat. Add minced garlic and cook for about 1 minute until fragrant.
- Add crushed tomatoes, salt, and pepper. Simmer for 15-20 minutes until the sauce thickens slightly. Remove from heat and let it cool.

3. Preheat and Prepare Pizza:

- Preheat your oven to its highest temperature (usually around 500°F or 260°C) and place a pizza stone or inverted baking sheet inside to heat.
- Punch down the dough and divide it into two equal portions. On a floured surface, stretch or roll out each portion into a circle (about 10-12 inches in diameter).

4. Assemble the Pizza:

- Place the stretched dough onto a piece of parchment paper.
- Spread half of the tomato sauce evenly over the dough, leaving a small border around the edges.
- Sprinkle half of the shredded mozzarella cheese evenly over the sauce.
- Distribute the chopped ham and pineapple chunks over the cheese.

5. Bake the Pizza:

- Using a pizza peel or inverted baking sheet, carefully transfer the pizza (with the parchment paper) onto the preheated pizza stone or baking sheet in the oven.
- Bake for 10-12 minutes, or until the crust is golden and the cheese is bubbly and slightly browned.

6. Finish and Serve:

- Remove the pizza from the oven and let it cool for a minute. Optionally, sprinkle with fresh basil leaves and red pepper flakes for extra flavor.
- Slice and serve hot.

Enjoy your homemade Hawaiian Pizza with its delicious blend of sweet pineapple and savory ham!

BBQ Chicken Pizza

Ingredients:

Pizza Dough:

- 1⅓ cups warm water (about 105°F or 40°C)
- 2¼ teaspoons active dry yeast (1 packet)
- 3½ cups all-purpose flour
- 2 tablespoons olive oil
- 1½ teaspoons salt
- 1 teaspoon sugar

Pizza Toppings:

- 1 cup cooked chicken breast, shredded or diced
- ½ cup barbecue sauce (choose your favorite flavor)
- 1 cup shredded mozzarella cheese
- ½ cup red onion, thinly sliced
- ¼ cup fresh cilantro, chopped (optional)
- Olive oil, for drizzling
- Cornmeal or flour, for dusting

Instructions:

1. Prepare the Dough:

- In a small bowl, combine warm water, yeast, and sugar. Let it sit for 5-10 minutes until foamy.
- In a large mixing bowl, combine flour and salt. Make a well in the center and add the yeast mixture and olive oil.
- Stir until a dough forms, then knead on a floured surface for about 5-7 minutes until smooth and elastic.
- Place dough in an oiled bowl, cover with a damp cloth, and let it rise in a warm place for about 1-2 hours until doubled in size.

2. Preheat and Prepare Pizza:

- Preheat your oven to its highest temperature (usually around 500°F or 260°C) and place a pizza stone or inverted baking sheet inside to heat.
- Punch down the dough and divide it into two equal portions. On a floured surface, stretch or roll out each portion into a circle (about 10-12 inches in diameter).

3. Assemble the Pizza:

- Place the stretched dough onto a piece of parchment paper dusted with cornmeal or flour.
- Spread half of the barbecue sauce evenly over the dough, leaving a small border around the edges.
- Sprinkle half of the shredded mozzarella cheese over the sauce.
- Distribute half of the shredded chicken and sliced red onion over the cheese.

4. Bake the Pizza:

- Using a pizza peel or inverted baking sheet, carefully transfer the pizza (with the parchment paper) onto the preheated pizza stone or baking sheet in the oven.
- Bake for 10-12 minutes, or until the crust is golden and the cheese is bubbly and slightly browned.

5. Finish and Serve:

- Remove the pizza from the oven and let it cool for a minute. Optionally, sprinkle with chopped cilantro and drizzle with a little olive oil for extra flavor.
- Slice and serve hot.

Enjoy your delicious homemade BBQ Chicken Pizza! The smoky barbecue sauce, tender chicken, and crisp crust make it a crowd-pleaser.

Supreme Pizza

Ingredients:

Pizza Dough:

- 1⅓ cups warm water (about 105°F or 40°C)
- 2¼ teaspoons active dry yeast (1 packet)
- 3½ cups all-purpose flour
- 2 tablespoons olive oil
- 1½ teaspoons salt
- 1 teaspoon sugar

Pizza Toppings:

- 1 cup pizza sauce (store-bought or homemade)
- 1½ cups shredded mozzarella cheese
- ½ cup sliced pepperoni
- ½ cup cooked Italian sausage, crumbled
- ½ cup sliced bell peppers (mix of red, green, and yellow)
- ½ cup sliced mushrooms
- ¼ cup sliced black olives
- ¼ cup thinly sliced red onion
- 1 tablespoon olive oil, for drizzling
- Fresh basil leaves, chopped (optional)
- Grated Parmesan cheese (optional)
- Red pepper flakes (optional)

Instructions:

1. Prepare the Dough:

- In a small bowl, combine warm water, yeast, and sugar. Let it sit for 5-10 minutes until foamy.
- In a large mixing bowl, combine flour and salt. Make a well in the center and add the yeast mixture and olive oil.
- Stir until a dough forms, then knead on a floured surface for about 5-7 minutes until smooth and elastic.
- Place dough in an oiled bowl, cover with a damp cloth, and let it rise in a warm place for about 1-2 hours until doubled in size.

2. Preheat and Prepare Pizza:

- Preheat your oven to its highest temperature (usually around 500°F or 260°C) and place a pizza stone or inverted baking sheet inside to heat.

- Punch down the dough and divide it into two equal portions. On a floured surface, stretch or roll out each portion into a circle (about 10-12 inches in diameter).

3. Assemble the Pizza:

- Place the stretched dough onto a piece of parchment paper.
- Spread half of the pizza sauce evenly over the dough, leaving a small border around the edges.
- Sprinkle half of the shredded mozzarella cheese evenly over the sauce.
- Evenly distribute the pepperoni, Italian sausage, bell peppers, mushrooms, black olives, and red onion over the cheese.

4. Bake the Pizza:

- Using a pizza peel or inverted baking sheet, carefully transfer the pizza (with the parchment paper) onto the preheated pizza stone or baking sheet in the oven.
- Bake for 10-12 minutes, or until the crust is golden and the cheese is bubbly and slightly browned.

5. Finish and Serve:

- Remove the pizza from the oven and let it cool for a minute. Drizzle with olive oil and sprinkle with chopped fresh basil, grated Parmesan cheese, and red pepper flakes if desired.
- Slice and serve hot.

Enjoy your homemade Supreme Pizza! It's packed with savory toppings and flavors that everyone will love.

Veggie Lover's Pizza

Ingredients:

Pizza Dough:

- 1⅓ cups warm water (about 105°F or 40°C)
- 2¼ teaspoons active dry yeast (1 packet)
- 3½ cups all-purpose flour
- 2 tablespoons olive oil
- 1½ teaspoons salt
- 1 teaspoon sugar

Pizza Toppings:

- 1 cup pizza sauce (store-bought or homemade)
- 1½ cups shredded mozzarella cheese
- ½ cup sliced bell peppers (mix of red, green, and yellow)
- ½ cup sliced mushrooms
- ½ cup sliced red onion
- ½ cup sliced black olives
- ½ cup chopped broccoli florets
- ½ cup chopped spinach
- ½ cup sliced cherry tomatoes
- 1 tablespoon olive oil, for drizzling
- Fresh basil leaves, chopped (optional)
- Grated Parmesan cheese (optional)
- Red pepper flakes (optional)

Instructions:

1. Prepare the Dough:

- In a small bowl, combine warm water, yeast, and sugar. Let it sit for 5-10 minutes until foamy.
- In a large mixing bowl, combine flour and salt. Make a well in the center and add the yeast mixture and olive oil.
- Stir until a dough forms, then knead on a floured surface for about 5-7 minutes until smooth and elastic.
- Place dough in an oiled bowl, cover with a damp cloth, and let it rise in a warm place for about 1-2 hours until doubled in size.

2. Preheat and Prepare Pizza:

- Preheat your oven to its highest temperature (usually around 500°F or 260°C) and place a pizza stone or inverted baking sheet inside to heat.
- Punch down the dough and divide it into two equal portions. On a floured surface, stretch or roll out each portion into a circle (about 10-12 inches in diameter).

3. Assemble the Pizza:

- Place the stretched dough onto a piece of parchment paper.
- Spread half of the pizza sauce evenly over the dough, leaving a small border around the edges.
- Sprinkle half of the shredded mozzarella cheese evenly over the sauce.
- Evenly distribute the sliced bell peppers, mushrooms, red onion, black olives, broccoli florets, spinach, and cherry tomatoes over the cheese.

4. Bake the Pizza:

- Using a pizza peel or inverted baking sheet, carefully transfer the pizza (with the parchment paper) onto the preheated pizza stone or baking sheet in the oven.
- Bake for 10-12 minutes, or until the crust is golden and the cheese is bubbly and slightly browned.

5. Finish and Serve:

- Remove the pizza from the oven and let it cool for a minute. Drizzle with olive oil and sprinkle with chopped fresh basil, grated Parmesan cheese, and red pepper flakes if desired.
- Slice and serve hot.

Enjoy your homemade Veggie Lover's Pizza! It's packed with delicious and nutritious vegetables for a satisfying meal. Adjust the toppings based on your preferences and enjoy the fresh flavors!

Meat Lover's Pizza

Ingredients:

Pizza Dough:

- 1⅓ cups warm water (about 105°F or 40°C)
- 2¼ teaspoons active dry yeast (1 packet)
- 3½ cups all-purpose flour
- 2 tablespoons olive oil
- 1½ teaspoons salt
- 1 teaspoon sugar

Pizza Toppings:

- 1 cup pizza sauce (store-bought or homemade)
- 1½ cups shredded mozzarella cheese
- ½ cup sliced pepperoni
- ½ cup cooked Italian sausage, crumbled
- ½ cup cooked bacon, chopped
- ½ cup sliced ham or Canadian bacon
- ¼ cup sliced black olives (optional)
- Fresh basil leaves, chopped (optional)
- Grated Parmesan cheese (optional)
- Red pepper flakes (optional)

Instructions:

1. Prepare the Dough:

- In a small bowl, combine warm water, yeast, and sugar. Let it sit for 5-10 minutes until foamy.
- In a large mixing bowl, combine flour and salt. Make a well in the center and add the yeast mixture and olive oil.
- Stir until a dough forms, then knead on a floured surface for about 5-7 minutes until smooth and elastic.
- Place dough in an oiled bowl, cover with a damp cloth, and let it rise in a warm place for about 1-2 hours until doubled in size.

2. Preheat and Prepare Pizza:

- Preheat your oven to its highest temperature (usually around 500°F or 260°C) and place a pizza stone or inverted baking sheet inside to heat.
- Punch down the dough and divide it into two equal portions. On a floured surface, stretch or roll out each portion into a circle (about 10-12 inches in diameter).

3. Assemble the Pizza:

- Place the stretched dough onto a piece of parchment paper.
- Spread half of the pizza sauce evenly over the dough, leaving a small border around the edges.
- Sprinkle half of the shredded mozzarella cheese evenly over the sauce.
- Evenly distribute the pepperoni, crumbled Italian sausage, chopped bacon, sliced ham or Canadian bacon, and black olives (if using) over the cheese.

4. Bake the Pizza:

- Using a pizza peel or inverted baking sheet, carefully transfer the pizza (with the parchment paper) onto the preheated pizza stone or baking sheet in the oven.
- Bake for 10-12 minutes, or until the crust is golden and the cheese is bubbly and slightly browned.

5. Finish and Serve:

- Remove the pizza from the oven and let it cool for a minute. Optionally, sprinkle with chopped fresh basil, grated Parmesan cheese, and red pepper flakes for extra flavor.
- Slice and serve hot.

Enjoy your homemade Meat Lover's Pizza! It's packed with savory meats and cheese, making it a perfect choice for pizza lovers who enjoy a hearty meal. Adjust the toppings according to your preferences and enjoy the delicious flavors!

Buffalo Chicken Pizza

Ingredients:

Pizza Dough:

- 1⅓ cups warm water (about 105°F or 40°C)
- 2¼ teaspoons active dry yeast (1 packet)
- 3½ cups all-purpose flour
- 2 tablespoons olive oil
- 1½ teaspoons salt
- 1 teaspoon sugar

Pizza Toppings:

- 1 cup cooked chicken breast, shredded or diced
- ½ cup buffalo sauce (adjust to taste)
- 1 cup shredded mozzarella cheese
- ½ cup crumbled blue cheese or Gorgonzola cheese
- ½ cup sliced red onion
- 2-3 tablespoons ranch or blue cheese dressing
- Fresh cilantro or parsley, chopped (optional)
- Olive oil, for drizzling
- Cornmeal or flour, for dusting

Instructions:

1. Prepare the Dough:

- In a small bowl, combine warm water, yeast, and sugar. Let it sit for 5-10 minutes until foamy.
- In a large mixing bowl, combine flour and salt. Make a well in the center and add the yeast mixture and olive oil.
- Stir until a dough forms, then knead on a floured surface for about 5-7 minutes until smooth and elastic.
- Place dough in an oiled bowl, cover with a damp cloth, and let it rise in a warm place for about 1-2 hours until doubled in size.

2. Preheat and Prepare Pizza:

- Preheat your oven to its highest temperature (usually around 500°F or 260°C) and place a pizza stone or inverted baking sheet inside to heat.
- Punch down the dough and divide it into two equal portions. On a floured surface, stretch or roll out each portion into a circle (about 10-12 inches in diameter).

3. Assemble the Pizza:

- Place the stretched dough onto a piece of parchment paper dusted with cornmeal or flour.
- In a bowl, toss the cooked chicken with buffalo sauce until evenly coated.
- Spread half of the ranch or blue cheese dressing evenly over the dough, leaving a small border around the edges.
- Sprinkle half of the shredded mozzarella cheese over the dressing.
- Evenly distribute the buffalo chicken mixture and sliced red onion over the cheese.
- Sprinkle crumbled blue cheese or Gorgonzola cheese on top.

4. Bake the Pizza:

- Using a pizza peel or inverted baking sheet, carefully transfer the pizza (with the parchment paper) onto the preheated pizza stone or baking sheet in the oven.
- Bake for 10-12 minutes, or until the crust is golden and the cheese is bubbly and slightly browned.

5. Finish and Serve:

- Remove the pizza from the oven and let it cool for a minute. Drizzle with a little olive oil and sprinkle with chopped fresh cilantro or parsley, if desired.
- Slice and serve hot.

Enjoy your homemade Buffalo Chicken Pizza! It's packed with spicy buffalo sauce, tender chicken, and creamy cheese for a delicious twist on traditional pizza. Adjust the sauce and cheese amounts according to your preference for an extra kick or creaminess!

White Pizza

Ingredients:

Pizza Dough:

- 1⅓ cups warm water (about 105°F or 40°C)
- 2¼ teaspoons active dry yeast (1 packet)
- 3½ cups all-purpose flour
- 2 tablespoons olive oil
- 1½ teaspoons salt
- 1 teaspoon sugar

White Pizza Sauce:

- 2 tablespoons unsalted butter
- 2 cloves garlic, minced
- 2 tablespoons all-purpose flour
- 1 cup whole milk
- ½ cup grated Parmesan cheese
- ½ teaspoon dried oregano
- Salt and pepper to taste

Pizza Toppings:

- 2 cups shredded mozzarella cheese
- ½ cup ricotta cheese
- ¼ cup grated Parmesan cheese
- Fresh basil leaves, chopped (optional)
- Red pepper flakes (optional)
- Olive oil, for drizzling

Instructions:

1. Prepare the Dough:

- In a small bowl, combine warm water, yeast, and sugar. Let it sit for 5-10 minutes until foamy.
- In a large mixing bowl, combine flour and salt. Make a well in the center and add the yeast mixture and olive oil.
- Stir until a dough forms, then knead on a floured surface for about 5-7 minutes until smooth and elastic.
- Place dough in an oiled bowl, cover with a damp cloth, and let it rise in a warm place for about 1-2 hours until doubled in size.

2. Prepare the White Pizza Sauce:

- In a medium saucepan, melt butter over medium heat. Add minced garlic and sauté for 1-2 minutes until fragrant.
- Stir in flour and cook for another 1-2 minutes until lightly golden.
- Gradually whisk in milk, stirring constantly, until mixture thickens and comes to a simmer.
- Remove from heat and stir in grated Parmesan cheese, dried oregano, salt, and pepper. Set aside.

3. Preheat and Prepare Pizza:

- Preheat your oven to its highest temperature (usually around 500°F or 260°C) and place a pizza stone or inverted baking sheet inside to heat.
- Punch down the dough and divide it into two equal portions. On a floured surface, stretch or roll out each portion into a circle (about 10-12 inches in diameter).

4. Assemble the Pizza:

- Place the stretched dough onto a piece of parchment paper dusted with cornmeal or flour.
- Spread half of the white pizza sauce evenly over the dough, leaving a small border around the edges.
- Sprinkle half of the shredded mozzarella cheese evenly over the sauce.
- Drop spoonfuls of ricotta cheese over the pizza.
- Sprinkle with grated Parmesan cheese.

5. Bake the Pizza:

- Using a pizza peel or inverted baking sheet, carefully transfer the pizza (with the parchment paper) onto the preheated pizza stone or baking sheet in the oven.
- Bake for 10-12 minutes, or until the crust is golden and the cheese is bubbly and slightly browned.

6. Finish and Serve:

- Remove the pizza from the oven and let it cool for a minute. Drizzle with a little olive oil and sprinkle with chopped fresh basil leaves and red pepper flakes, if desired.
- Slice and serve hot.

Enjoy your homemade White Pizza! It's creamy, cheesy, and flavorful, perfect for those who prefer a pizza without tomato sauce. Adjust the cheese and toppings according to your taste, and savor the deliciousness!

Pesto Chicken Pizza

Ingredients:

- 1 pre-made pizza dough (or homemade if preferred)
- 1/2 cup basil pesto (store-bought or homemade)
- 1 cup cooked chicken breast, shredded or diced
- 1 cup shredded mozzarella cheese
- 1/2 cup cherry tomatoes, halved
- 1/4 cup red onion, thinly sliced
- 1/4 cup black olives, sliced (optional)
- Fresh basil leaves, for garnish
- Salt and pepper, to taste
- Olive oil, for drizzling

Instructions:

1. **Preheat the Oven**: Preheat your oven to the temperature specified on your pizza dough package, usually around 425°F (220°C).
2. **Prepare the Pizza Dough**: Roll out the pizza dough on a floured surface to your desired thickness. Place it on a pizza stone or baking sheet lined with parchment paper.
3. **Spread the Pesto**: Spread the basil pesto evenly over the pizza dough, leaving a small border around the edges for the crust.
4. **Add the Toppings**: Evenly distribute the shredded chicken, mozzarella cheese, cherry tomatoes, red onion slices, and black olives (if using) over the pesto-covered dough.
5. **Season**: Sprinkle salt and pepper over the pizza according to your taste.
6. **Bake the Pizza**: Place the pizza in the preheated oven and bake according to the pizza dough package instructions, typically 12-15 minutes or until the crust is golden and the cheese is melted and bubbly.
7. **Finish and Serve**: Once baked, remove the pizza from the oven. Drizzle a little olive oil over the top and garnish with fresh basil leaves for extra flavor and freshness.
8. **Slice and Enjoy**: Slice the pizza into wedges or squares and serve hot.

Tips:

- **Homemade Pesto**: To make homemade pesto, blend fresh basil leaves, garlic, pine nuts (or walnuts), Parmesan cheese, salt, and olive oil until smooth.
- **Chicken**: You can use leftover grilled or roasted chicken for this recipe. Season it with salt, pepper, and a bit of garlic powder before adding to the pizza.
- **Variations**: Feel free to add other toppings like mushrooms, bell peppers, or artichoke hearts to suit your taste.

Enjoy your delicious Pesto Chicken Pizza!

Mediterranean Pizza

Ingredients:

- 1 pre-made pizza dough (or homemade if preferred)
- 1/2 cup tomato sauce or marinara sauce
- 1 cup shredded mozzarella cheese
- 1/2 cup crumbled feta cheese
- 1/4 cup sliced black olives
- 1/4 cup sliced sun-dried tomatoes (packed in oil, drained)
- 1/4 cup sliced red onion
- 1/4 cup chopped artichoke hearts (canned or marinated)
- 1/4 cup chopped fresh basil leaves
- 1 tablespoon olive oil
- 1 teaspoon dried oregano
- Salt and pepper, to taste

Instructions:

1. **Preheat the Oven**: Preheat your oven to the temperature specified on your pizza dough package, typically around 425°F (220°C).
2. **Prepare the Pizza Dough**: Roll out the pizza dough on a floured surface to your desired thickness. Place it on a pizza stone or baking sheet lined with parchment paper.
3. **Spread the Sauce**: Spread the tomato sauce evenly over the pizza dough, leaving a small border around the edges for the crust.
4. **Add the Cheeses**: Sprinkle the shredded mozzarella cheese evenly over the sauce. Then, distribute the crumbled feta cheese on top.
5. **Add the Toppings**: Evenly distribute the black olives, sun-dried tomatoes, sliced red onion, and chopped artichoke hearts over the cheese.
6. **Season and Drizzle**: Sprinkle dried oregano, salt, and pepper over the pizza according to your taste. Drizzle olive oil over the top for added flavor.
7. **Bake the Pizza**: Place the pizza in the preheated oven and bake according to the pizza dough package instructions, usually 12-15 minutes or until the crust is golden and the cheese is melted and bubbly.
8. **Finish and Serve**: Once baked, remove the pizza from the oven. Sprinkle chopped fresh basil leaves over the top for a burst of freshness.
9. **Slice and Enjoy**: Slice the pizza into wedges or squares and serve hot.

Tips:

- **Variations**: You can customize this pizza with additional Mediterranean ingredients such as roasted red peppers, Kalamata olives, or even a drizzle of balsamic glaze after baking.

- **Dough Options**: If you prefer a thinner crust, you can roll the dough out more thinly. Alternatively, for a thicker crust, use a smaller baking sheet or pizza stone to create a deeper dish.

This Mediterranean Pizza is perfect for a flavorful and satisfying meal, bringing together the delicious tastes of the Mediterranean region. Enjoy!

Caprese Pizza

Ingredients:

- 1 pre-made pizza dough (or homemade if preferred)
- 1/2 cup tomato sauce or marinara sauce
- 2 cups fresh mozzarella cheese, sliced or shredded
- 2-3 medium tomatoes, thinly sliced
- 1/2 cup fresh basil leaves, torn or chopped
- 2-3 cloves garlic, minced
- 2 tablespoons balsamic glaze (store-bought or homemade)
- Salt and pepper, to taste
- Olive oil, for drizzling

Instructions:

1. **Preheat the Oven**: Preheat your oven to the temperature specified on your pizza dough package, typically around 425°F (220°C).
2. **Prepare the Pizza Dough**: Roll out the pizza dough on a floured surface to your desired thickness. Place it on a pizza stone or baking sheet lined with parchment paper.
3. **Spread the Sauce**: Spread the tomato sauce evenly over the pizza dough, leaving a small border around the edges for the crust.
4. **Add the Mozzarella**: Distribute the sliced or shredded mozzarella cheese evenly over the sauce.
5. **Layer the Tomatoes and Basil**: Arrange the thinly sliced tomatoes over the cheese. Sprinkle minced garlic evenly over the tomatoes. Scatter torn or chopped fresh basil leaves on top.
6. **Season**: Sprinkle salt and pepper over the pizza according to your taste.
7. **Bake the Pizza**: Place the pizza in the preheated oven and bake according to the pizza dough package instructions, usually 12-15 minutes or until the crust is golden and the cheese is melted and bubbly.
8. **Finish and Drizzle**: Once baked, remove the pizza from the oven. Drizzle balsamic glaze over the top for extra flavor.
9. **Slice and Serve**: Slice the pizza into wedges or squares and serve hot. Optionally, drizzle a little olive oil over the top before serving for added richness.

Tips:

- **Fresh Ingredients**: The key to a great Caprese Pizza is using fresh and high-quality ingredients, especially the mozzarella, tomatoes, and basil.
- **Balsamic Glaze**: If you don't have balsamic glaze, you can reduce balsamic vinegar with a bit of sugar over low heat until it thickens to a syrupy consistency.
- **Variations**: For a twist, you can add prosciutto or grilled chicken slices for a heartier version.

This Caprese Pizza is perfect for summer evenings or anytime you crave the fresh flavors of tomatoes, mozzarella, and basil. Enjoy!

Four Cheese Pizza

Ingredients:

- 1 pre-made pizza dough (or homemade if preferred)
- 1/2 cup tomato sauce or marinara sauce
- 1 cup shredded mozzarella cheese
- 1/2 cup shredded cheddar cheese
- 1/2 cup shredded provolone cheese
- 1/2 cup crumbled feta cheese
- 1-2 cloves garlic, minced (optional)
- Fresh basil leaves, chopped, for garnish
- Red pepper flakes (optional)
- Olive oil, for drizzling

Instructions:

1. **Preheat the Oven**: Preheat your oven to the temperature specified on your pizza dough package, typically around 425°F (220°C).
2. **Prepare the Pizza Dough**: Roll out the pizza dough on a floured surface to your desired thickness. Place it on a pizza stone or baking sheet lined with parchment paper.
3. **Spread the Sauce**: Spread the tomato sauce evenly over the pizza dough, leaving a small border around the edges for the crust.
4. **Add the Cheeses**: Sprinkle the shredded mozzarella cheese, cheddar cheese, provolone cheese, and crumbled feta cheese evenly over the sauce. Spread minced garlic evenly over the cheeses if using.
5. **Bake the Pizza**: Place the pizza in the preheated oven and bake according to the pizza dough package instructions, usually 12-15 minutes or until the crust is golden and the cheese is melted and bubbly.
6. **Finish and Garnish**: Once baked, remove the pizza from the oven. Drizzle a little olive oil over the top. Garnish with chopped fresh basil leaves and red pepper flakes for added flavor and color.
7. **Slice and Serve**: Slice the pizza into wedges or squares and serve hot.

Tips:

- **Cheese Options**: Feel free to mix and match your favorite cheeses for this pizza. Other great options include Gouda, Fontina, or Asiago.
- **Garlic**: If you love garlic, adding minced garlic between the sauce and cheese layers can elevate the flavor of the pizza.
- **Variations**: You can add toppings like sliced mushrooms, caramelized onions, or sliced bell peppers to customize your Four Cheese Pizza.

This Four Cheese Pizza is sure to satisfy any cheese lover's craving with its gooey, melty goodness. Enjoy!

Sausage and Mushroom Pizza

Ingredients:

- 1 pre-made pizza dough (or homemade if preferred)
- 1/2 cup tomato sauce or marinara sauce
- 1 cup shredded mozzarella cheese
- 1/2 cup sliced mushrooms (cremini or button mushrooms)
- 1/2 cup cooked sausage, crumbled or sliced (Italian sausage or your favorite variety)
- 1/4 cup sliced black olives (optional)
- 1/4 cup sliced red onion (optional)
- Fresh basil leaves, chopped, for garnish
- Olive oil, for drizzling
- Salt and pepper, to taste
- Red pepper flakes (optional)

Instructions:

1. **Preheat the Oven**: Preheat your oven to the temperature specified on your pizza dough package, typically around 425°F (220°C).
2. **Prepare the Pizza Dough**: Roll out the pizza dough on a floured surface to your desired thickness. Place it on a pizza stone or baking sheet lined with parchment paper.
3. **Spread the Sauce**: Spread the tomato sauce evenly over the pizza dough, leaving a small border around the edges for the crust.
4. **Add the Cheese and Toppings**: Sprinkle the shredded mozzarella cheese evenly over the sauce. Arrange the sliced mushrooms and cooked sausage (crumbled or sliced) over the cheese. If using, add sliced black olives and red onion.
5. **Season**: Season with salt and pepper according to your taste preference. Optionally, sprinkle red pepper flakes for added heat.
6. **Drizzle with Olive Oil**: Drizzle a little olive oil over the pizza for extra flavor.
7. **Bake the Pizza**: Place the pizza in the preheated oven and bake according to the pizza dough package instructions, usually 12-15 minutes or until the crust is golden and the cheese is melted and bubbly.
8. **Finish and Garnish**: Once baked, remove the pizza from the oven. Sprinkle chopped fresh basil leaves over the top for a burst of freshness.
9. **Slice and Serve**: Slice the pizza into wedges or squares and serve hot.

Tips:

- **Variations**: You can customize this pizza by using different types of sausage (e.g., spicy sausage, chicken sausage) or adding other toppings like bell peppers or spinach.
- **Pre-cooking Toppings**: If using raw mushrooms or other vegetables, consider sautéing them lightly before adding to the pizza for enhanced flavor.

- **Cheese Blend**: For extra flavor, mix in a bit of shredded Parmesan cheese with the mozzarella.

This Sausage and Mushroom Pizza is perfect for a satisfying meal, whether for a casual dinner or a gathering with friends. Enjoy the savory combination of sausage, mushrooms, and cheese on a crispy crust!

Spinach and Feta Pizza

Ingredients:

- 1 pre-made pizza dough (or homemade if preferred)
- 1/2 cup tomato sauce or marinara sauce
- 1 cup shredded mozzarella cheese
- 1 cup fresh spinach leaves, washed and dried
- 1/2 cup crumbled feta cheese
- 1/4 cup sliced black olives (optional)
- 1/4 cup sliced red onion (optional)
- 1-2 cloves garlic, minced

Sure, here's a simple and delicious recipe for Spinach and Feta Pizza:

Ingredients:

- 1 pre-made pizza dough (or homemade if preferred)
- 1/2 cup tomato sauce or marinara sauce
- 1 cup shredded mozzarella cheese
- 1 cup fresh spinach leaves, washed and dried
- 1/2 cup crumbled feta cheese
- 1/4 cup sliced black olives (optional)
- 1/4 cup sliced red onion (optional)
- 1-2 cloves garlic, minced
- Olive oil, for drizzling
- Salt and pepper, to taste
- Red pepper flakes, for garnish (optional)

Instructions:

1. **Preheat the Oven**: Preheat your oven to the temperature specified on your pizza dough package, typically around 425°F (220°C).
2. **Prepare the Pizza Dough**: Roll out the pizza dough on a floured surface to your desired thickness. Place it on a pizza stone or baking sheet lined with parchment paper.
3. **Spread the Sauce**: Spread the tomato sauce evenly over the pizza dough, leaving a small border around the edges for the crust.
4. **Add the Mozzarella Cheese**: Sprinkle the shredded mozzarella cheese evenly over the sauce.
5. **Add the Spinach**: Evenly distribute the fresh spinach leaves over the cheese. If the leaves are large, tear them into smaller pieces.
6. **Crumble the Feta Cheese**: Sprinkle the crumbled feta cheese over the spinach.
7. **Add Optional Toppings**: If using, scatter sliced black olives and red onion over the pizza.

8. **Season and Drizzle with Olive Oil**: Sprinkle minced garlic evenly over the pizza. Season with salt and pepper to taste. Drizzle a little olive oil over the top.
9. **Bake the Pizza**: Place the pizza in the preheated oven and bake according to the pizza dough package instructions, usually 12-15 minutes or until the crust is golden and the cheese is melted and bubbly.
10. **Finish and Serve**: Once baked, remove the pizza from the oven. Optionally, sprinkle red pepper flakes over the top for a bit of spice.
11. **Slice and Enjoy**: Slice the pizza into wedges or squares and serve hot.

Tips:

- **Variations**: You can add other vegetables such as sliced cherry tomatoes or bell peppers to enhance the flavors and colors of the pizza.
- **Fresh Ingredients**: Use fresh spinach for the best flavor and texture. You can also use baby spinach leaves if preferred.
- **Garlic**: If you love garlic, feel free to adjust the amount to suit your taste. You can also sauté the minced garlic briefly in olive oil before spreading it on the pizza for a milder flavor.

This Spinach and Feta Pizza is a great choice for a vegetarian meal or as part of a pizza night with friends and family. Enjoy the combination of creamy feta cheese and fresh spinach on a crispy pizza crust!

Taco Pizza

Ingredients:

- 1 pre-made pizza dough (or homemade if preferred)
- 1/2 cup refried beans
- 1/2 cup salsa
- 1 cup cooked ground beef or turkey, seasoned with taco seasoning
- 1 cup shredded Mexican cheese blend (cheddar, Monterey Jack, etc.)
- 1/2 cup shredded lettuce
- 1/2 cup diced tomatoes
- 1/4 cup sliced black olives
- 1/4 cup sliced jalapeños (optional)
- 1/4 cup chopped fresh cilantro
- Sour cream, for serving
- Sliced avocado or guacamole, for serving
- Lime wedges, for serving

Instructions:

1. **Preheat the Oven**: Preheat your oven to the temperature specified on your pizza dough package, typically around 425°F (220°C).
2. **Prepare the Pizza Dough**: Roll out the pizza dough on a floured surface to your desired thickness. Place it on a pizza stone or baking sheet lined with parchment paper.
3. **Spread the Refried Beans**: Spread the refried beans evenly over the pizza dough, leaving a small border around the edges for the crust.
4. **Spread the Salsa**: Spread the salsa over the refried beans.
5. **Add the Cooked Meat**: Evenly distribute the cooked ground beef or turkey seasoned with taco seasoning over the salsa.
6. **Sprinkle with Cheese**: Sprinkle the shredded Mexican cheese blend evenly over the pizza.
7. **Add Toppings**: Scatter shredded lettuce, diced tomatoes, sliced black olives, and sliced jalapeños (if using) over the cheese.
8. **Bake the Pizza**: Place the pizza in the preheated oven and bake according to the pizza dough package instructions, usually 12-15 minutes or until the crust is golden and the cheese is melted and bubbly.
9. **Finish and Garnish**: Once baked, remove the pizza from the oven. Sprinkle chopped fresh cilantro over the top.
10. **Serve**: Slice the Taco Pizza into wedges and serve hot. Serve with sour cream, sliced avocado or guacamole, and lime wedges on the side.

Tips:

- **Taco Seasoning**: You can use store-bought taco seasoning or make your own blend using chili powder, cumin, paprika, garlic powder, onion powder, oregano, salt, and pepper.
- **Variations**: Customize your Taco Pizza with additional toppings such as sliced bell peppers, red onions, or even black beans.
- **Crust Options**: For a crispier crust, pre-bake the pizza dough for a few minutes before adding the toppings.
- **Freshness**: Add fresh ingredients like lettuce, tomatoes, and cilantro after baking for a vibrant, crisp texture.

This Taco Pizza is perfect for a fun and flavorful meal that combines the best of tacos and pizza. Enjoy the delicious fusion of flavors!

Philly Cheesesteak Pizza

Ingredients:

- 1 pre-made pizza dough (or homemade if preferred)
- 1/2 cup pizza sauce or marinara sauce
- 1 cup shredded provolone cheese
- 1 cup shredded mozzarella cheese
- 1 green bell pepper, thinly sliced
- 1/2 onion, thinly sliced
- 8 ounces thinly sliced steak (such as ribeye or sirloin)
- Salt and pepper, to taste
- Olive oil, for cooking
- 1 tablespoon butter
- 1-2 cloves garlic, minced
- Fresh parsley, chopped, for garnish

Instructions:

1. **Preheat the Oven**: Preheat your oven to the temperature specified on your pizza dough package, typically around 425°F (220°C).
2. **Prepare the Pizza Dough**: Roll out the pizza dough on a floured surface to your desired thickness. Place it on a pizza stone or baking sheet lined with parchment paper.
3. **Cook the Steak**: Heat a large skillet over medium-high heat. Add a drizzle of olive oil. Season the thinly sliced steak with salt and pepper. Cook the steak slices for 2-3 minutes per side until browned and cooked to your liking. Remove the steak from the skillet and set aside.
4. **Cook the Vegetables**: In the same skillet, melt the butter over medium heat. Add the thinly sliced bell pepper and onion. Cook, stirring occasionally, until the vegetables are softened and slightly caramelized, about 5-7 minutes. Add minced garlic in the last minute of cooking. Remove from heat.
5. **Assemble the Pizza**: Spread pizza sauce evenly over the pizza dough, leaving a small border around the edges for the crust. Sprinkle shredded provolone cheese evenly over the sauce. Spread the cooked bell pepper and onion mixture over the cheese. Arrange the cooked steak slices evenly over the vegetables. Top with shredded mozzarella cheese.
6. **Bake the Pizza**: Place the pizza in the preheated oven and bake according to the pizza dough package instructions, usually 12-15 minutes or until the crust is golden and the cheese is melted and bubbly.
7. **Finish and Garnish**: Once baked, remove the pizza from the oven. Sprinkle chopped fresh parsley over the top for a burst of freshness.
8. **Slice and Serve**: Slice the Philly Cheesesteak Pizza into wedges and serve hot.

Tips:

- **Cheese**: Provolone is traditional for Philly cheesesteaks, but you can also use a blend of provolone and mozzarella for extra gooeyness.
- **Variations**: Customize your Philly Cheesesteak Pizza with additional toppings like mushrooms, banana peppers, or even a drizzle of cheese sauce.
- **Steak**: Thinly slicing the steak ensures it cooks quickly and evenly on the pizza. You can also use leftover grilled steak or roast beef if preferred.

This Philly Cheesesteak Pizza is perfect for satisfying your cravings for both pizza and Philly cheesesteak sandwiches. Enjoy the savory flavors and cheesy goodness!

Breakfast Pizza

Ingredients:

- 1 pre-made pizza dough (or homemade if preferred)
- 1 tablespoon olive oil
- 1 cup shredded mozzarella cheese
- 4 large eggs
- 4 slices bacon, cooked and crumbled
- 1/2 cup diced ham
- 1/2 cup diced bell peppers (any color)
- 1/4 cup sliced mushrooms
- 1/4 cup diced red onion
- Salt and pepper, to taste
- Fresh parsley or chives, chopped, for garnish

Instructions:

1. **Preheat the Oven**: Preheat your oven to the temperature specified on your pizza dough package, typically around 425°F (220°C).
2. **Prepare the Pizza Dough**: Roll out the pizza dough on a floured surface to your desired thickness. Place it on a pizza stone or baking sheet lined with parchment paper.
3. **Pre-cook the Dough (optional)**: If you prefer a crispier crust, you can pre-bake the pizza dough for 5-7 minutes before adding toppings. This step is optional but recommended for a crisper crust.
4. **Assemble the Pizza**:
    - Brush olive oil evenly over the pizza dough.
    - Sprinkle shredded mozzarella cheese over the dough.
    - Evenly distribute cooked and crumbled bacon, diced ham, diced bell peppers, sliced mushrooms, and diced red onion over the cheese.
5. **Crack and Add Eggs**: Carefully crack the eggs onto the pizza, spacing them evenly apart. You can crack them directly onto the pizza or crack them into a small bowl first and then gently pour them onto the pizza.
6. **Season**: Season with salt and pepper to taste.
7. **Bake the Pizza**: Place the pizza in the preheated oven and bake for 12-15 minutes, or until the crust is golden brown and the egg whites are set. The egg yolks should still be slightly runny for a perfect breakfast pizza.
8. **Finish and Garnish**: Remove the pizza from the oven. Sprinkle chopped fresh parsley or chives over the top for a pop of color and freshness.
9. **Slice and Serve**: Slice the Breakfast Pizza into wedges or squares and serve hot.

Tips:

- **Variations**: Feel free to customize your Breakfast Pizza with additional toppings such as spinach, tomatoes, sausage, or different types of cheese like cheddar or feta.
- **Egg Cooking**: If you prefer well-cooked eggs, you can beat the eggs before pouring them onto the pizza. Alternatively, you can crack the eggs directly onto the pizza for sunny-side-up style eggs.
- **Crust Options**: Experiment with different types of pizza crusts such as whole wheat or cauliflower crust for a healthier option.

This Breakfast Pizza is a versatile dish that can be enjoyed for brunch or any time you're craving a hearty breakfast in pizza form. Enjoy the combination of flavors and textures!

Chicken Alfredo Pizza

Ingredients:

- 1 pre-made pizza dough (or homemade if preferred)
- 1 cup cooked chicken breast, shredded or diced
- 1 cup Alfredo sauce (store-bought or homemade)
- 1 cup shredded mozzarella cheese
- 1/2 cup shredded Parmesan cheese
- 1/4 cup sliced sun-dried tomatoes (packed in oil, drained)
- 1/4 cup chopped fresh spinach
- 2 cloves garlic, minced
- 1/2 teaspoon dried oregano
- Salt and pepper, to taste
- Fresh basil leaves, chopped, for garnish
- Olive oil, for drizzling

Instructions:

1. **Preheat the Oven**: Preheat your oven to the temperature specified on your pizza dough package, typically around 425°F (220°C).
2. **Prepare the Pizza Dough**: Roll out the pizza dough on a floured surface to your desired thickness. Place it on a pizza stone or baking sheet lined with parchment paper.
3. **Spread the Alfredo Sauce**: Spread the Alfredo sauce evenly over the pizza dough, leaving a small border around the edges for the crust.
4. **Add the Cooked Chicken**: Evenly distribute the shredded or diced cooked chicken breast over the Alfredo sauce.
5. **Sprinkle with Cheeses**: Sprinkle shredded mozzarella cheese and shredded Parmesan cheese evenly over the pizza.
6. **Add Toppings**: Scatter sliced sun-dried tomatoes, chopped fresh spinach, and minced garlic over the cheese. Season with dried oregano, salt, and pepper to taste.
7. **Drizzle with Olive Oil**: Drizzle a little olive oil over the top of the pizza for added flavor.
8. **Bake the Pizza**: Place the pizza in the preheated oven and bake according to the pizza dough package instructions, usually 12-15 minutes or until the crust is golden and the cheese is melted and bubbly.
9. **Finish and Garnish**: Once baked, remove the pizza from the oven. Sprinkle chopped fresh basil leaves over the top for a burst of freshness.
10. **Slice and Serve**: Slice the Chicken Alfredo Pizza into wedges or squares and serve hot.

Tips:

- **Alfredo Sauce**: You can use store-bought Alfredo sauce for convenience or make your own by combining butter, cream, garlic, and Parmesan cheese.

- **Chicken**: Season the chicken with salt, pepper, and any other desired herbs or spices before cooking for added flavor.
- **Variations**: Add other toppings such as mushrooms, caramelized onions, or cooked bacon to suit your taste preferences.
- **Crust Options**: Experiment with different types of pizza crusts such as whole wheat or gluten-free crusts.

This Chicken Alfredo Pizza is creamy, flavorful, and perfect for a cozy dinner or a special occasion. Enjoy the indulgent combination of Alfredo sauce, chicken, and cheese on a crispy pizza crust!

Shrimp Scampi Pizza

Ingredients:

- 1 pre-made pizza dough (or homemade if preferred)
- 1/2 cup unsalted butter
- 4 cloves garlic, minced
- 1/4 cup white wine (optional)
- 1 pound large shrimp, peeled and deveined
- Salt and pepper, to taste
- 1 cup shredded mozzarella cheese
- 1/4 cup grated Parmesan cheese
- 1/4 cup chopped fresh parsley
- Red pepper flakes, for garnish (optional)
- Olive oil, for drizzling
- Lemon wedges, for serving

Instructions:

1. **Preheat the Oven**: Preheat your oven to the temperature specified on your pizza dough package, typically around 425°F (220°C).
2. **Prepare the Pizza Dough**: Roll out the pizza dough on a floured surface to your desired thickness. Place it on a pizza stone or baking sheet lined with parchment paper.
3. **Prepare the Shrimp Scampi**:
    - In a large skillet, melt the butter over medium heat.
    - Add minced garlic and sauté for 1-2 minutes until fragrant.
    - If using, pour in the white wine and let it simmer for another minute.
    - Add the shrimp to the skillet and season with salt and pepper. Cook the shrimp for 2-3 minutes per side until pink and cooked through. Remove from heat.
4. **Assemble the Pizza**:
    - Spread the cooked shrimp scampi mixture evenly over the pizza dough.
    - Sprinkle shredded mozzarella cheese and grated Parmesan cheese over the shrimp.
5. **Bake the Pizza**: Place the pizza in the preheated oven and bake according to the pizza dough package instructions, usually 12-15 minutes or until the crust is golden and the cheese is melted and bubbly.
6. **Finish and Garnish**:
    - Once baked, remove the pizza from the oven.
    - Sprinkle chopped fresh parsley over the top for a pop of color and freshness.
    - Optionally, sprinkle red pepper flakes over the pizza for added heat.
7. **Drizzle with Olive Oil**: Drizzle a little olive oil over the pizza for extra flavor.
8. **Serve**: Slice the Shrimp Scampi Pizza into wedges and serve hot with lemon wedges on the side for squeezing over the pizza.

Tips:

- **Garlic Butter**: The key to delicious shrimp scampi is a flavorful garlic butter sauce. Adjust the amount of garlic according to your preference.
- **Wine**: White wine adds depth to the shrimp scampi sauce, but you can omit it if preferred or substitute with chicken broth.
- **Fresh Ingredients**: Use fresh shrimp for the best flavor and texture. You can also add other toppings such as sliced cherry tomatoes or baby spinach for variation.
- **Crust Options**: Experiment with different types of pizza crusts such as whole wheat or gluten-free crusts.

This Shrimp Scampi Pizza is perfect for seafood lovers and makes a delightful dish for a special dinner or a weekend treat. Enjoy the combination of tender shrimp, garlic butter sauce, and cheese on a crispy pizza crust!

Artichoke and Spinach Pizza

Ingredients:

- 1 pre-made pizza dough (or homemade if preferred)
- 1/2 cup Alfredo sauce (store-bought or homemade)
- 1 cup shredded mozzarella cheese
- 1 cup chopped spinach (fresh or frozen, thawed and drained)
- 1 cup chopped canned artichoke hearts, drained
- 1/4 cup grated Parmesan cheese
- 1/4 teaspoon garlic powder
- Red pepper flakes, to taste (optional)
- Olive oil, for drizzling
- Salt and pepper, to taste

Instructions:

1. **Preheat the Oven**: Preheat your oven to the temperature specified on your pizza dough package, typically around 425°F (220°C).
2. **Prepare the Pizza Dough**: Roll out the pizza dough on a floured surface to your desired thickness. Place it on a pizza stone or baking sheet lined with parchment paper.
3. **Spread the Alfredo Sauce**: Spread the Alfredo sauce evenly over the pizza dough, leaving a small border around the edges for the crust.
4. **Add the Spinach and Artichokes**: Evenly distribute the chopped spinach and chopped artichoke hearts over the Alfredo sauce.
5. **Sprinkle with Cheeses and Seasonings**: Sprinkle shredded mozzarella cheese and grated Parmesan cheese over the toppings. Season with garlic powder, salt, and pepper to taste. Optionally, add red pepper flakes for a hint of spice.
6. **Drizzle with Olive Oil**: Drizzle a little olive oil over the top of the pizza for added flavor.
7. **Bake the Pizza**: Place the pizza in the preheated oven and bake according to the pizza dough package instructions, usually 12-15 minutes or until the crust is golden and the cheese is melted and bubbly.
8. **Finish and Serve**: Once baked, remove the pizza from the oven. Allow it to cool slightly before slicing. Optionally, garnish with fresh basil leaves or additional grated Parmesan cheese before serving.

Tips:

- **Variations**: Add other toppings such as sliced cherry tomatoes or black olives for additional flavor and color.
- **Alfredo Sauce**: You can use store-bought Alfredo sauce for convenience or make your own by combining butter, cream, garlic, and Parmesan cheese.
- **Fresh vs. Frozen Spinach**: If using frozen spinach, make sure to thaw and drain it well to remove excess moisture before using it on the pizza.

- **Crust Options**: Experiment with different types of pizza crusts such as whole wheat or gluten-free crusts.

This Artichoke and Spinach Pizza is a delightful combination of creamy Alfredo sauce, tender spinach, and tangy artichokes, all on a crispy pizza crust. Enjoy this vegetarian pizza as a delicious meal for lunch or dinner!

Prosciutto and Arugula Pizza

Ingredients:

- 1 pre-made pizza dough (or homemade if preferred)
- 1/2 cup pizza sauce or marinara sauce
- 1 cup shredded mozzarella cheese
- 4-6 slices of prosciutto
- 1 cup fresh arugula
- 1/4 cup shaved Parmesan cheese
- Olive oil, for drizzling
- Salt and pepper, to taste
- Red pepper flakes (optional)
- Balsamic glaze, for drizzling (optional)

Instructions:

1. **Preheat the Oven**: Preheat your oven to the temperature specified on your pizza dough package, typically around 425°F (220°C).
2. **Prepare the Pizza Dough**: Roll out the pizza dough on a floured surface to your desired thickness. Place it on a pizza stone or baking sheet lined with parchment paper.
3. **Spread the Sauce**: Spread the pizza sauce evenly over the pizza dough, leaving a small border around the edges for the crust.
4. **Add the Mozzarella Cheese**: Sprinkle shredded mozzarella cheese evenly over the sauce.
5. **Arrange Prosciutto**: Tear or arrange the slices of prosciutto evenly over the cheese.
6. **Bake the Pizza**: Place the pizza in the preheated oven and bake according to the pizza dough package instructions, usually 12-15 minutes or until the crust is golden and the cheese is melted and bubbly.
7. **Add Arugula and Parmesan**: Remove the pizza from the oven. While still hot, scatter fresh arugula over the top. The heat of the pizza will slightly wilt the arugula.
8. **Drizzle with Olive Oil and Season**: Drizzle a little olive oil over the arugula. Season with salt and pepper to taste. Optionally, sprinkle red pepper flakes for a hint of spice.
9. **Finish with Parmesan and Balsamic Glaze**: Shave or sprinkle shaved Parmesan cheese over the pizza. Optionally, drizzle with balsamic glaze for added sweetness and depth of flavor.
10. **Slice and Serve**: Slice the Prosciutto and Arugula Pizza into wedges and serve hot.

Tips:

- **Cheese**: If you prefer more cheese, you can add additional Parmesan or even a bit of goat cheese for extra creaminess.
- **Arugula**: Use fresh arugula for the best flavor and texture. Baby arugula works well too.

- **Variations**: You can enhance the flavor by adding sliced cherry tomatoes, caramelized onions, or a sprinkle of pine nuts before baking.
- **Crust Options**: Experiment with different types of pizza crusts such as whole wheat or gluten-free crusts.

This Prosciutto and Arugula Pizza is perfect for a light and flavorful meal. Enjoy the combination of salty prosciutto, peppery arugula, and cheesy goodness on a crispy pizza crust!

Truffle Oil Pizza

Ingredients:

- 1 pre-made pizza dough (or homemade if preferred)
- 1/2 cup pizza sauce or marinara sauce
- 1 cup shredded mozzarella cheese
- 1/4 cup grated Parmesan cheese
- 2 tablespoons truffle oil
- 1/4 cup sliced mushrooms (such as cremini or button)
- 1/4 cup sliced red onion
- Fresh arugula, for garnish
- Salt and pepper, to taste
- Red pepper flakes (optional)

Instructions:

1. **Preheat the Oven**: Preheat your oven to the temperature specified on your pizza dough package, typically around 425°F (220°C).
2. **Prepare the Pizza Dough**: Roll out the pizza dough on a floured surface to your desired thickness. Place it on a pizza stone or baking sheet lined with parchment paper.
3. **Spread the Sauce**: Spread the pizza sauce evenly over the pizza dough, leaving a small border around the edges for the crust.
4. **Add the Mozzarella Cheese**: Sprinkle shredded mozzarella cheese evenly over the sauce.
5. **Drizzle with Truffle Oil**: Drizzle truffle oil evenly over the cheese and sauce. Use a light hand as truffle oil is potent in flavor.
6. **Add Toppings**: Scatter sliced mushrooms and sliced red onion over the pizza.
7. **Season**: Season with salt and pepper to taste. Optionally, sprinkle red pepper flakes for a hint of spice.
8. **Bake the Pizza**: Place the pizza in the preheated oven and bake according to the pizza dough package instructions, usually 12-15 minutes or until the crust is golden and the cheese is melted and bubbly.
9. **Finish and Garnish**: Once baked, remove the pizza from the oven. Top with fresh arugula for a peppery freshness.
10. **Slice and Serve**: Slice the Truffle Oil Pizza into wedges and serve hot.

Tips:

- **Truffle Oil**: Use high-quality truffle oil for the best flavor. Truffle oil is strong, so a little goes a long way.
- **Cheese**: Experiment with adding different cheeses such as goat cheese or fontina to complement the truffle flavor.

- **Variations**: Add cooked crumbled sausage, prosciutto, or caramelized onions for additional depth of flavor.
- **Crust Options**: Try different types of pizza crusts like thin crust or whole wheat for variation.

This Truffle Oil Pizza is perfect for those who enjoy the luxurious flavor of truffles. Enjoy the earthy aroma and rich taste of truffle oil combined with savory toppings on a freshly baked pizza crust!

Bacon and Egg Pizza

Ingredients:

- 1 pre-made pizza dough (or homemade if preferred)
- 1/2 cup pizza sauce or marinara sauce
- 1 cup shredded mozzarella cheese
- 4-6 slices of bacon, cooked and crumbled
- 4 large eggs
- 1/4 cup grated Parmesan cheese
- Fresh chives or green onions, chopped, for garnish
- Salt and pepper, to taste
- Red pepper flakes (optional)

Instructions:

1. **Preheat the Oven**: Preheat your oven to the temperature specified on your pizza dough package, typically around 425°F (220°C).
2. **Prepare the Pizza Dough**: Roll out the pizza dough on a floured surface to your desired thickness. Place it on a pizza stone or baking sheet lined with parchment paper.
3. **Spread the Sauce**: Spread the pizza sauce evenly over the pizza dough, leaving a small border around the edges for the crust.
4. **Add the Mozzarella Cheese**: Sprinkle shredded mozzarella cheese evenly over the sauce.
5. **Arrange Bacon**: Evenly distribute the cooked and crumbled bacon over the cheese.
6. **Crack and Add Eggs**: Carefully crack the eggs onto the pizza, spacing them evenly apart. Try to keep the yolks intact.
7. **Season**: Season with salt and pepper to taste. Sprinkle grated Parmesan cheese over the top.
8. **Bake the Pizza**: Place the pizza in the preheated oven and bake according to the pizza dough package instructions, usually 12-15 minutes or until the crust is golden and the cheese is melted and bubbly, and the egg whites are set.
9. **Finish and Garnish**: Once baked, remove the pizza from the oven. Sprinkle chopped fresh chives or green onions over the top for a burst of freshness. Optionally, sprinkle red pepper flakes for a bit of heat.
10. **Slice and Serve**: Slice the Bacon and Egg Pizza into wedges and serve hot.

Tips:

- **Eggs**: If you prefer well-cooked eggs, you can beat the eggs before pouring them onto the pizza. Alternatively, crack the eggs directly onto the pizza for sunny-side-up style eggs.
- **Variations**: Add sliced cherry tomatoes, caramelized onions, or a sprinkle of feta cheese for added flavor.

- **Crust Options**: Experiment with different types of pizza crusts such as whole wheat or gluten-free crusts.
- **Bacon**: For a smokier flavor, you can use smoked bacon or pancetta.

This Bacon and Egg Pizza is a satisfying and flavorful meal that combines the classic breakfast combination of bacon and eggs with the convenience of pizza. Enjoy it for brunch, lunch, or dinner!

Cauliflower Crust Pizza

Ingredients:

- 1 medium head of cauliflower, riced (about 4 cups of cauliflower rice)
- 1/2 cup shredded mozzarella cheese
- 1/4 cup grated Parmesan cheese
- 1/2 teaspoon dried oregano
- 1/2 teaspoon dried basil
- 1/2 teaspoon garlic powder
- 1/4 teaspoon salt
- 1/4 teaspoon black pepper
- 1 large egg
- Olive oil, for drizzling
- 1/2 cup pizza sauce or marinara sauce
- 1 cup shredded mozzarella cheese (for topping)
- Your choice of pizza toppings (e.g., pepperoni, mushrooms, bell peppers, spinach, etc.)
- Fresh basil or parsley, chopped, for garnish (optional)

Instructions:

1. **Preheat the Oven**: Preheat your oven to 400°F (200°C). Line a baking sheet with parchment paper.
2. **Prepare the Cauliflower**: Wash and dry the cauliflower head. Remove the leaves and core. Cut the cauliflower into florets. Place the florets in a food processor and pulse until you get fine cauliflower "rice." You should have about 4 cups of cauliflower rice.
3. **Cook the Cauliflower**: Place the cauliflower rice in a microwave-safe bowl and microwave on high for 5-6 minutes, stirring halfway through. Let it cool for a few minutes.
4. **Make the Cauliflower Crust**:
    - Transfer the cooked cauliflower rice to a clean kitchen towel or cheesecloth. Squeeze out as much liquid as possible. This step is crucial to ensure a crispy crust.
    - In a mixing bowl, combine the cauliflower rice, shredded mozzarella cheese, grated Parmesan cheese, dried oregano, dried basil, garlic powder, salt, and black pepper. Mix well.
    - Add the egg to the cauliflower mixture and mix until everything is combined.
5. **Form the Crust**:
    - Transfer the cauliflower mixture onto the prepared baking sheet lined with parchment paper. Using your hands, spread the mixture into a circle or rectangle, about 1/4 inch thick, to form the pizza crust.
6. **Bake the Crust**: Bake the cauliflower crust in the preheated oven for 20-25 minutes, or until golden and firm to the touch.
7. **Prepare the Pizza**:
    - Remove the crust from the oven and let it cool for a few minutes.

- Increase the oven temperature to 450°F (230°C).
- Drizzle olive oil over the crust and spread pizza sauce evenly over the crust.
- Sprinkle shredded mozzarella cheese over the sauce.
- Add your choice of pizza toppings over the cheese.

8. **Bake the Pizza**: Return the pizza to the oven and bake for an additional 10-15 minutes, or until the cheese is melted and bubbly.
9. **Finish and Garnish**: Once baked, remove the pizza from the oven. Sprinkle chopped fresh basil or parsley over the top for a burst of freshness.
10. **Slice and Serve**: Slice the Cauliflower Crust Pizza into wedges or squares and serve hot.

Tips:

- **Toppings**: Customize your pizza with your favorite toppings. Keep in mind that adding too many toppings can make the crust soggy, so use them sparingly.
- **Crust Texture**: For a crispier crust, ensure you squeeze out as much moisture as possible from the cauliflower after cooking.
- **Storage**: Leftovers can be stored in an airtight container in the refrigerator for 2-3 days. Reheat in the oven or toaster oven for best results.

This Cauliflower Crust Pizza is a nutritious and delicious alternative to traditional pizza crusts, perfect for those looking to reduce carbs or avoid gluten. Enjoy the crispy crust and flavorful toppings!

Gluten-Free Pizza

Ingredients:

- 1 cup gluten-free all-purpose flour blend
- 1 teaspoon baking powder
- 1/2 teaspoon salt
- 1/2 teaspoon Italian seasoning (optional)
- 1/2 cup plain Greek yogurt
- 1 large egg
- 1 tablespoon olive oil

Instructions:

1. **Preheat the Oven**: Preheat your oven to 425°F (220°C). Line a baking sheet with parchment paper.
2. **Mix Dry Ingredients**: In a mixing bowl, whisk together the gluten-free flour blend, baking powder, salt, and Italian seasoning (if using).
3. **Add Wet Ingredients**: Add the Greek yogurt, egg, and olive oil to the dry ingredients. Mix until a dough forms. If the dough is too sticky, add a little more flour. If it's too dry, add a teaspoon of water at a time until you achieve a smooth dough.
4. **Form the Crust**: Transfer the dough to the prepared baking sheet. Using your hands or a rolling pin, flatten and shape the dough into a round pizza crust or desired shape, about 1/4 inch thick.
5. **Bake the Crust**: Bake the crust in the preheated oven for 10-12 minutes, or until it begins to turn golden brown.
6. **Prepare the Pizza**: Remove the crust from the oven and top it with your favorite pizza sauce, cheese, and toppings.
7. **Bake the Pizza**: Return the pizza to the oven and bake for an additional 10-15 minutes, or until the cheese is melted and bubbly and the crust is fully cooked.
8. **Serve**: Slice and serve hot.

Topping Ideas for Gluten-Free Pizza:

- **Classic Margherita**: Tomato sauce, fresh mozzarella cheese, fresh basil leaves, and a drizzle of olive oil.
- **Vegetarian**: Pesto sauce, cherry tomatoes, spinach, mushrooms, and goat cheese.
- **Meat Lovers**: BBQ sauce, cooked chicken, red onions, bell peppers, and cheddar cheese.
- **Mediterranean**: Hummus or olive tapenade, roasted vegetables (like bell peppers, zucchini, and eggplant), feta cheese, and fresh herbs.
- **Caprese**: Tomato slices, fresh mozzarella, basil leaves, and a balsamic glaze drizzle.

Tips:

- **Flour Blends**: Use a pre-made gluten-free all-purpose flour blend for convenience, or make your own using a combination of rice flour, tapioca flour, and potato starch.
- **Dough Texture**: Gluten-free dough tends to be stickier than traditional dough. Use oiled hands or a lightly floured surface to handle it.
- **Baking Time**: Keep an eye on the pizza while baking, as gluten-free crusts may bake faster than wheat-based crusts.
- **Crust Thickness**: Adjust the thickness of the crust to your preference. Thinner crusts will bake faster and be crispier, while thicker crusts will be softer.

By following this recipe and using your favorite toppings, you can create a delicious gluten-free pizza that everyone will enjoy, whether they are avoiding gluten or not!

Deep Dish Pizza

Ingredients:

- 3 cups all-purpose flour
- 1/4 cup cornmeal
- 1 tablespoon sugar
- 1 teaspoon salt
- 1 packet (2 1/4 teaspoons) instant yeast
- 1 1/4 cups warm water (about 110°F/45°C)
- 1/4 cup olive oil
- 1 tablespoon melted butter, for greasing the pan

Instructions:

1. **Prepare the Dough**:
   - In a large mixing bowl, combine the flour, cornmeal, sugar, salt, and yeast.
   - Add the warm water and olive oil to the dry ingredients. Mix until a dough forms.
   - Turn the dough out onto a lightly floured surface and knead for about 5 minutes, until smooth and elastic.
2. **First Rise**:
   - Place the dough in a greased bowl, turning once to coat. Cover with a clean kitchen towel or plastic wrap.
   - Let the dough rise in a warm place for about 1 hour, or until doubled in size.
3. **Prepare the Pan**:
   - While the dough is rising, grease a 12-inch round deep dish pizza pan or a cast iron skillet with the melted butter.
4. **Shape the Dough**:
   - Punch down the risen dough and transfer it to the prepared pizza pan.
   - Use your hands to press the dough evenly across the bottom and up the sides of the pan, forming a thick crust.
5. **Second Rise**:
   - Cover the pan with a kitchen towel and let the dough rise again for about 30 minutes.

Deep Dish Pizza Assembly:

Ingredients:

- Prepared deep dish pizza dough
- 2 cups shredded mozzarella cheese
- 1 cup pizza sauce or marinara sauce
- Your choice of toppings (e.g., pepperoni, cooked sausage, bell peppers, onions, mushrooms, etc.)
- Grated Parmesan cheese, for sprinkling

- Fresh basil leaves, chopped, for garnish (optional)

Instructions:

1. **Preheat the Oven**: Preheat your oven to 425°F (220°C).
2. **Layer the Cheese and Toppings**:
    - Sprinkle half of the shredded mozzarella cheese over the dough in the pizza pan.
    - Layer your chosen toppings evenly over the cheese.
    - Spoon the pizza sauce or marinara sauce over the toppings, spreading it out with the back of a spoon.
3. **Final Cheese Layer**:
    - Sprinkle the remaining shredded mozzarella cheese over the sauce.
4. **Bake the Pizza**:
    - Place the pizza in the preheated oven and bake for 25-30 minutes, or until the crust is golden brown and the cheese is bubbly and lightly browned.
5. **Finish and Serve**:
    - Remove the pizza from the oven and let it cool in the pan for a few minutes.
    - Sprinkle grated Parmesan cheese and chopped fresh basil over the top for extra flavor and freshness.
    - Slice the Deep Dish Pizza into wedges and serve hot.

Tips:

- **Toppings**: Choose toppings that won't release too much moisture during baking to prevent the crust from becoming soggy.
- **Pan Options**: If you don't have a deep dish pizza pan, you can use a cast iron skillet or a regular baking dish, adjusting the amount of dough and toppings accordingly.
- **Crust Thickness**: Adjust the thickness of the crust to your preference by pressing the dough thinner or thicker on the sides and bottom of the pan.

This Deep Dish Pizza recipe yields a thick, hearty pizza with a crispy crust and plenty of room for your favorite toppings. Enjoy the rich flavors and satisfying texture of a homemade deep dish pizza!

Thin Crust Pizza

Ingredients:

- 2 1/2 cups all-purpose flour
- 1 teaspoon sugar
- 1 teaspoon salt
- 1 tablespoon olive oil
- 1 cup warm water (about 110°F/45°C)
- 1 packet (2 1/4 teaspoons) instant yeast

Instructions:

1. **Mix Dough**:
   - In a large mixing bowl, combine the flour, sugar, and salt.
   - Add the olive oil and warm water to the dry ingredients. Mix until a dough forms.
   - Turn the dough out onto a lightly floured surface and knead for about 5 minutes, until smooth and elastic.
2. **First Rise**:
   - Place the dough in a greased bowl, turning once to coat. Cover with a clean kitchen towel or plastic wrap.
   - Let the dough rise in a warm place for about 1 hour, or until doubled in size.
3. **Preheat Oven**:
   - Preheat your oven to the highest temperature setting available (typically around 500°F/260°C). If using a pizza stone, place it in the oven to preheat as well.
4. **Roll Out Dough**:
   - Once risen, punch down the dough and divide it into two equal portions for two pizzas.
   - On a lightly floured surface, roll out each portion of dough into a thin circle or rectangle, about 1/8 inch thick. Use a rolling pin to achieve an even thickness.
5. **Prepare Pizza**:
   - Transfer the rolled-out dough to a piece of parchment paper or a pizza peel dusted with cornmeal (for easy transfer to the oven).

Thin Crust Pizza Assembly:

Ingredients:

- Thin crust pizza dough (prepared)
- 1/2 cup pizza sauce or marinara sauce
- 1 1/2 cups shredded mozzarella cheese
- Your choice of toppings (e.g., pepperoni, sliced bell peppers, onions, mushrooms, etc.)
- Olive oil, for drizzling
- Fresh basil leaves, chopped, for garnish (optional)
- Red pepper flakes (optional)

- Grated Parmesan cheese (optional)

Instructions:

1. **Add Sauce and Cheese:**
   - Spread the pizza sauce evenly over the prepared dough, leaving a small border around the edges.
   - Sprinkle shredded mozzarella cheese over the sauce.
2. **Add Toppings:**
   - Arrange your chosen toppings evenly over the cheese. Less is more for a thin crust pizza to prevent it from becoming soggy.
3. **Drizzle with Olive Oil:**
   - Drizzle a little olive oil over the toppings for extra flavor and to help them cook and brown.
4. **Bake the Pizza:**
   - Slide the pizza (on the parchment paper or pizza peel) onto the preheated pizza stone or baking sheet in the oven.
   - Bake for 10-12 minutes, or until the crust is golden brown and the cheese is melted and bubbly.
5. **Finish and Serve:**
   - Remove the pizza from the oven and let it cool for a minute or two.
   - Sprinkle chopped fresh basil leaves, red pepper flakes, and grated Parmesan cheese over the top if desired.
   - Slice the Thin Crust Pizza into wedges and serve hot.

Tips:

- **High Temperature**: Preheating the oven to a high temperature ensures a crispy crust. Keep an eye on the pizza to prevent burning.
- **Toppings**: Choose toppings that cook quickly, as the pizza bakes for a short time at a high temperature.
- **Pizza Stone**: Using a pizza stone helps create an evenly heated surface, resulting in a crispier crust.
- **Variations**: Experiment with different sauces (like pesto or BBQ sauce) and toppings to create unique flavor combinations.

This Thin Crust Pizza recipe provides a crispy, flavorful base for your favorite toppings. Enjoy making and customizing this classic pizza style at home!

Stuffed Crust Pizza

Ingredients:

- 3 cups all-purpose flour
- 1 teaspoon sugar
- 1 teaspoon salt
- 1 tablespoon olive oil
- 1 cup warm water (about 110°F/45°C)
- 1 packet (2 1/4 teaspoons) instant yeast

Cheese Filling:

- 8 ounces low-moisture mozzarella cheese, string cheese, or cheese sticks

Instructions:

1. **Mix Dough**:
   - In a large mixing bowl, combine the flour, sugar, and salt.
   - Add the olive oil and warm water to the dry ingredients. Mix until a dough forms.
   - Turn the dough out onto a lightly floured surface and knead for about 5 minutes, until smooth and elastic.
2. **First Rise**:
   - Place the dough in a greased bowl, turning once to coat. Cover with a clean kitchen towel or plastic wrap.
   - Let the dough rise in a warm place for about 1 hour, or until doubled in size.
3. **Preheat Oven**:
   - Preheat your oven to the highest temperature setting available (typically around 500°F/260°C). If using a pizza stone, place it in the oven to preheat as well.
4. **Prepare Cheese Filling**:
   - While the dough is rising, cut the mozzarella cheese into sticks or chunks, depending on the size of your crust and personal preference.
5. **Form the Crust**:
   - Divide the risen dough in half. Roll out one portion of the dough into a circle or rectangle, about 1/4 inch thick, on a lightly floured surface.
6. **Add Cheese Filling**:
   - Arrange the mozzarella cheese sticks or chunks around the edge of the dough, leaving a small border.
7. **Seal and Shape**:
   - Fold the edge of the dough over the cheese filling and pinch the edges to seal. Roll the sealed edge gently to even it out and ensure the cheese is securely enclosed.

Assembling and Baking:

Ingredients:

- Prepared stuffed crust pizza dough
- 1/2 cup pizza sauce or marinara sauce
- 1 1/2 cups shredded mozzarella cheese
- Your choice of toppings (e.g., pepperoni, sliced bell peppers, onions, mushrooms, etc.)
- Olive oil, for drizzling
- Fresh basil leaves, chopped, for garnish (optional)
- Red pepper flakes (optional)
- Grated Parmesan cheese (optional)

Instructions:

1. **Add Sauce and Toppings**:
    - Spread the pizza sauce evenly over the prepared dough, including inside the stuffed crust.
2. **Sprinkle Cheese and Toppings**:
    - Sprinkle shredded mozzarella cheese over the sauce and toppings, covering the entire pizza.
3. **Drizzle with Olive Oil**:
    - Drizzle a little olive oil over the cheese and toppings for extra flavor and to help them cook and brown.
4. **Bake the Pizza**:
    - Slide the pizza onto the preheated pizza stone or baking sheet in the oven.
    - Bake for 12-15 minutes, or until the crust is golden brown and the cheese is melted and bubbly.
5. **Finish and Serve**:
    - Remove the pizza from the oven and let it cool for a minute or two.
    - Sprinkle chopped fresh basil leaves, red pepper flakes, and grated Parmesan cheese over the top if desired.
    - Slice the Stuffed Crust Pizza into wedges and serve hot.

Tips:

- **Cheese Filling**: Experiment with different cheeses for the stuffed crust, such as cheddar, pepper jack, or provolone, for different flavors.
- **Toppings**: Customize your pizza with your favorite toppings. Ensure they are cooked or sliced thinly to ensure even baking.
- **Variations**: Add garlic butter or herbs to the crust before baking for additional flavor.
- **Handling the Dough**: Handle the dough gently when forming and stretching to avoid tearing the crust.

This Stuffed Crust Pizza recipe creates a deliciously cheesy and indulgent pizza that is sure to satisfy your cravings. Enjoy making and savoring this special pizza treat at home!

Sicilian Pizza

Ingredients:

- 4 cups bread flour
- 1 1/2 cups warm water (about 110°F/45°C)
- 2 1/4 teaspoons instant yeast (1 packet)
- 2 tablespoons olive oil
- 2 teaspoons sugar
- 1 teaspoon salt

Instructions:

1. **Proof the Yeast**:
    - In a small bowl, combine the warm water, sugar, and yeast. Let it sit for about 5-10 minutes, until foamy.
2. **Mix Dough**:
    - In a large mixing bowl or the bowl of a stand mixer fitted with a dough hook, combine the flour and salt.
    - Add the proofed yeast mixture and olive oil to the flour mixture. Mix until a dough starts to come together.
3. **Knead Dough**:
    - Knead the dough by hand on a lightly floured surface or with a stand mixer for about 8-10 minutes, until smooth and elastic. Add more flour if the dough is too sticky.
4. **First Rise**:
    - Place the dough in a greased bowl, turning once to coat. Cover with plastic wrap or a kitchen towel.
    - Let the dough rise in a warm place for about 1-2 hours, until doubled in size.

Assembling and Baking Sicilian Pizza:

Ingredients:

- Prepared Sicilian pizza dough
- 1/4 cup olive oil, divided
- 1 can (15 ounces) crushed tomatoes or tomato sauce
- 1 teaspoon dried oregano
- 1 teaspoon dried basil
- Salt and pepper, to taste
- 1 cup shredded mozzarella cheese
- 1/4 cup grated Parmesan cheese
- Optional toppings: sliced onions, anchovies, breadcrumbs, olives, etc.

Instructions:

1. **Preheat Oven**:
    - Preheat your oven to 425°F (220°C). Lightly oil a large rimmed baking sheet (approximately 18x13 inches) with 2 tablespoons of olive oil.
2. **Prepare the Dough**:
    - Gently stretch and press the risen dough into the oiled baking sheet, covering the entire surface. If the dough resists, let it rest for a few minutes to relax before continuing to stretch.
3. **Top the Pizza**:
    - Drizzle the remaining 2 tablespoons of olive oil over the dough, spreading it evenly with your hands.
    - Spread the crushed tomatoes or tomato sauce evenly over the dough, leaving a small border around the edges.
    - Sprinkle dried oregano, dried basil, salt, and pepper over the sauce.
4. **Add Cheese and Toppings**:
    - Sprinkle shredded mozzarella cheese evenly over the sauce.
    - Add any desired toppings such as sliced onions, anchovies, olives, or breadcrumbs.
5. **Bake the Pizza**:
    - Bake in the preheated oven for 20-25 minutes, or until the crust is golden brown and the cheese is bubbly and lightly browned.
6. **Finish and Serve**:
    - Remove the Sicilian Pizza from the oven and let it cool in the pan for a few minutes.
    - Sprinkle grated Parmesan cheese over the top.
    - Cut into squares and serve hot, optionally garnished with fresh basil leaves.

Tips:

- **Dough Thickness**: The dough should be spread evenly across the baking sheet, but it will rise during baking to create a thick crust.
- **Toppings**: Traditional Sicilian Pizza toppings are simple and rustic. Adjust toppings according to your preference.
- **Baking Sheet Size**: Ensure your baking sheet is large enough to accommodate the dough and toppings without overcrowding.

Enjoy this authentic Sicilian Pizza recipe, which captures the flavors and textures of this classic Italian dish right in your own kitchen!

Neapolitan Pizza

Ingredients:

- 3 cups Italian "00" flour (or bread flour)
- 1 teaspoon salt
- 1 teaspoon sugar
- 1 packet (2 1/4 teaspoons) instant yeast
- 1 cup lukewarm water (about 110°F/45°C)
- 2 tablespoons olive oil

Instructions:

1. **Proof the Yeast:**
   - In a small bowl, combine the lukewarm water, sugar, and yeast. Let it sit for about 5-10 minutes, until foamy.
2. **Mix Dough:**
   - In a large mixing bowl or the bowl of a stand mixer fitted with a dough hook, combine the flour and salt.
   - Add the proofed yeast mixture and olive oil to the flour mixture. Mix until a dough starts to come together.
3. **Knead Dough:**
   - Knead the dough by hand on a lightly floured surface or with a stand mixer for about 8-10 minutes, until smooth and elastic. Add more flour if the dough is too sticky.
4. **First Rise:**
   - Place the dough in a lightly oiled bowl, turning once to coat. Cover with plastic wrap or a kitchen towel.
   - Let the dough rise in a warm place for about 1-2 hours, until doubled in size.

Assembling and Baking Neapolitan Pizza:

Ingredients:

- Prepared Neapolitan pizza dough
- 1/2 cup pizza sauce (preferably San Marzano tomatoes)
- 8 ounces fresh mozzarella cheese, sliced or torn into small pieces
- Fresh basil leaves, torn
- Olive oil, for drizzling
- Salt and pepper, to taste

Instructions:

1. **Preheat Oven:**

- Place a pizza stone or inverted baking sheet on the middle rack of your oven. Preheat the oven to its highest temperature setting, typically around 500°F (260°C), for at least 30 minutes to ensure the pizza stone is fully heated.
2. **Prepare Pizza**:
    - Once the dough has risen, punch it down and divide it into two equal portions.
    - On a lightly floured surface, gently stretch and shape each portion of dough into a round or oval shape, about 10-12 inches in diameter. Transfer the shaped dough to a piece of parchment paper.
3. **Top the Pizza**:
    - Spread half of the pizza sauce evenly over each pizza dough, leaving a small border around the edges.
    - Distribute the fresh mozzarella cheese pieces evenly over the sauce.
    - Tear fresh basil leaves and scatter them over the cheese.
    - Drizzle a little olive oil over the top and season with salt and pepper to taste.
4. **Bake the Pizza**:
    - Using a pizza peel or the back of a baking sheet, carefully transfer the pizza (with the parchment paper) onto the preheated pizza stone or inverted baking sheet in the oven.
    - Bake for 8-10 minutes, or until the crust is golden brown and the cheese is bubbly and lightly browned.
5. **Finish and Serve**:
    - Remove the Neapolitan Pizza from the oven and let it cool for a minute or two.
    - Optionally, garnish with additional fresh basil leaves and a drizzle of olive oil.
    - Slice and serve hot.

Tips:

- **High Temperature**: Preheating the oven and using a pizza stone or inverted baking sheet helps mimic the intense heat of a wood-fired oven, crucial for achieving a crispy crust.
- **Sauce and Cheese**: Use high-quality ingredients like San Marzano tomatoes for the sauce and fresh mozzarella cheese for the authentic Neapolitan flavor.
- **Handling the Dough**: Handle the dough gently to avoid deflating the air bubbles that contribute to the crust's texture.

Enjoy this homemade Neapolitan Pizza with its deliciously thin and chewy crust, classic tomato sauce, fresh mozzarella, and fragrant basil—perfect for a taste of Naples right in your own kitchen!

Chicago-style Deep Dish Pizza

Ingredients:

- 3 1/4 cups all-purpose flour
- 1/2 cup yellow cornmeal
- 1 tablespoon sugar
- 1 1/2 teaspoons salt
- 1 packet (2 1/4 teaspoons) instant yeast
- 1 1/4 cups lukewarm water (about 110°F/45°C)
- 1/4 cup unsalted butter, melted
- 1/4 cup olive oil

Instructions:

1. **Proof the Yeast**:
   - In a small bowl, combine the lukewarm water, sugar, and yeast. Let it sit for about 5-10 minutes, until foamy.
2. **Mix Dough**:
   - In a large mixing bowl or the bowl of a stand mixer fitted with a dough hook, combine the flour, cornmeal, and salt.
   - Add the proofed yeast mixture, melted butter, and olive oil to the flour mixture. Mix until a dough starts to come together.
3. **Knead Dough**:
   - Knead the dough by hand on a lightly floured surface or with a stand mixer for about 5-7 minutes, until smooth and elastic. Add more flour if the dough is too sticky.
4. **First Rise**:
   - Place the dough in a lightly oiled bowl, turning once to coat. Cover with plastic wrap or a kitchen towel.
   - Let the dough rise in a warm place for about 1-2 hours, until doubled in size.

Assembling and Baking Chicago-style Deep Dish Pizza:

Ingredients:

- Prepared Chicago-style deep dish pizza dough
- 1 lb mozzarella cheese, sliced or shredded
- 1 lb Italian sausage, cooked and crumbled (optional)
- 1 cup chunky tomato sauce or crushed tomatoes
- 1/2 cup grated Parmesan cheese
- 1/4 cup olive oil
- 1 teaspoon dried oregano
- Optional toppings: sliced bell peppers, onions, mushrooms, etc.

Instructions:

1. **Preheat Oven:**
   - Preheat your oven to 425°F (220°C). Lightly grease a 12-inch cast iron skillet or deep dish pizza pan with olive oil.
2. **Prepare Dough and Crust:**
   - Punch down the risen dough and divide it into two equal portions for two pizzas.
   - On a lightly floured surface, roll out one portion of dough into a circle or oval shape, about 1/4 inch thick. Transfer it to the prepared skillet or pan, pressing it evenly across the bottom and up the sides.
3. **Layer Cheese and Toppings:**
   - Layer half of the mozzarella cheese evenly over the dough.
   - Add cooked Italian sausage (if using) over the cheese.
   - Spread chunky tomato sauce or crushed tomatoes evenly over the sausage.
   - Sprinkle grated Parmesan cheese over the sauce.
   - Add any optional toppings such as sliced bell peppers, onions, or mushrooms.
4. **Top and Bake:**
   - Roll out the second portion of dough and place it over the toppings.
   - Press the edges of the top and bottom crusts together to seal, and fold overhanging dough inward to create a thick edge.
   - Drizzle olive oil over the top crust and sprinkle with dried oregano.
5. **Bake the Pizza:**
   - Bake in the preheated oven for 25-30 minutes, or until the crust is golden brown and the cheese is bubbly and lightly browned.
6. **Finish and Serve:**
   - Remove the pizza from the oven and let it cool in the pan for a few minutes.
   - Carefully transfer the pizza to a cutting board. Slice into wedges and serve hot.

Tips:

- **Pan Choice**: A 12-inch cast iron skillet or deep dish pizza pan is ideal for Chicago-style deep dish pizza, as it helps achieve a crispy crust.
- **Cheese**: Use slices or shredded mozzarella for a gooey, cheesy texture.
- **Toppings**: Customize your pizza with your favorite toppings, but keep in mind the layers—start with cheese, then meat (if using), followed by sauce and toppings.
- **Baking Time**: Adjust baking time as needed, ensuring the crust is fully cooked and golden brown.

Enjoy this homemade Chicago-style Deep Dish Pizza with its thick, buttery crust and layers of savory toppings—perfect for a hearty and satisfying pizza night!

Detroit-style Pizza

Ingredients:

- 3 1/2 cups bread flour
- 1 1/2 cups lukewarm water (about 110°F/45°C)
- 1 packet (2 1/4 teaspoons) instant yeast
- 1 tablespoon sugar
- 1 teaspoon salt
- 2 tablespoons olive oil
- 2 tablespoons unsalted butter, melted

Instructions:

1. **Proof the Yeast:**
   - In a small bowl, combine the lukewarm water, sugar, and yeast. Let it sit for about 5-10 minutes, until foamy.
2. **Mix Dough:**
   - In a large mixing bowl or the bowl of a stand mixer fitted with a dough hook, combine the bread flour and salt.
   - Add the proofed yeast mixture, olive oil, and melted butter to the flour mixture. Mix until a dough starts to come together.
3. **Knead Dough:**
   - Knead the dough by hand on a lightly floured surface or with a stand mixer for about 5-7 minutes, until smooth and elastic. Add more flour if the dough is too sticky.
4. **First Rise:**
   - Place the dough in a lightly oiled bowl, turning once to coat. Cover with plastic wrap or a kitchen towel.
   - Let the dough rise in a warm place for about 1-2 hours, until doubled in size.

Assembling and Baking Detroit-style Pizza:

Ingredients:

- Prepared Detroit-style pizza dough
- 1 cup shredded mozzarella cheese
- 1 cup shredded brick or aged cheddar cheese
- 1 cup tomato sauce or pizza sauce
- 1/2 cup grated Parmesan cheese
- 1/4 cup olive oil
- Optional toppings: pepperoni, cooked sausage, diced bell peppers, onions, mushrooms, etc.

Instructions:

1. **Preheat Oven**:
    - Preheat your oven to 450°F (230°C). Lightly grease a 9x13-inch rectangular baking pan with olive oil.
2. **Prepare Dough and Pan**:
    - Gently stretch and press the risen dough into the prepared baking pan, covering the entire surface. If the dough resists, let it rest for a few minutes to relax before continuing to stretch.
3. **Layer Cheese and Toppings**:
    - Evenly sprinkle shredded mozzarella cheese over the dough.
    - Spread tomato sauce or pizza sauce evenly over the cheese.
    - Sprinkle shredded brick or aged cheddar cheese over the sauce.
    - Add optional toppings such as pepperoni, cooked sausage, diced bell peppers, onions, or mushrooms.
4. **Bake the Pizza**:
    - Drizzle olive oil evenly over the top of the pizza.
    - Bake in the preheated oven for 20-25 minutes, or until the crust is golden brown and the cheese is bubbly and lightly browned.
5. **Finish and Serve**:
    - Remove the Detroit-style Pizza from the oven and let it cool in the pan for a few minutes.
    - Sprinkle grated Parmesan cheese over the top.
    - Cut into squares and serve hot.

Tips:

- **Cheese**: The combination of mozzarella and brick or aged cheddar cheese is traditional for Detroit-style pizza, contributing to its unique flavor and texture.
- **Toppings**: Customize your pizza with your favorite toppings, ensuring they are cooked or sliced thinly to ensure even baking.
- **Baking Time**: Adjust baking time as needed, ensuring the crust is fully cooked and golden brown.

Enjoy this homemade Detroit-style Pizza with its crispy edges, airy interior, and layers of cheesy goodness—perfect for a satisfying pizza night at home!

Calzone

Ingredients:

- 2 1/4 cups all-purpose flour
- 1 teaspoon salt
- 1 teaspoon sugar
- 1 packet (2 1/4 teaspoons) instant yeast
- 3/4 cup lukewarm water (about 110°F/45°C)
- 1 tablespoon olive oil

Instructions:

1. **Proof the Yeast:**
    - In a small bowl, combine the lukewarm water, sugar, and yeast. Let it sit for about 5-10 minutes, until foamy.
2. **Mix Dough:**
    - In a large mixing bowl or the bowl of a stand mixer fitted with a dough hook, combine the flour and salt.
    - Add the proofed yeast mixture and olive oil to the flour mixture. Mix until a dough starts to come together.
3. **Knead Dough:**
    - Knead the dough by hand on a lightly floured surface or with a stand mixer for about 5-7 minutes, until smooth and elastic. Add more flour if the dough is too sticky.
4. **First Rise:**
    - Place the dough in a lightly oiled bowl, turning once to coat. Cover with plastic wrap or a kitchen towel.
    - Let the dough rise in a warm place for about 1 hour, or until doubled in size.

Calzone Filling:

Ingredients:

- 1 cup ricotta cheese
- 1 cup shredded mozzarella cheese
- 1/2 cup grated Parmesan cheese
- 1/2 cup marinara sauce
- 1/2 cup sliced pepperoni or cooked Italian sausage (optional)
- 1/4 cup chopped fresh basil
- Salt and pepper, to taste

Instructions:

1. **Prepare Filling:**

- In a bowl, combine ricotta cheese, mozzarella cheese, Parmesan cheese, marinara sauce, pepperoni or sausage (if using), and chopped fresh basil. Season with salt and pepper to taste. Mix well.
2. **Assemble Calzone**:
    - Preheat your oven to 425°F (220°C). Line a baking sheet with parchment paper.
    - Punch down the risen dough and divide it into two equal portions.
    - On a lightly floured surface, roll out each portion of dough into a circle or oval shape, about 10-12 inches in diameter.
3. **Fill and Fold**:
    - Spread half of the filling mixture evenly on one half of each dough round, leaving a border around the edge.
    - Fold the other half of the dough over the filling to create a half-moon shape. Press the edges firmly to seal.
4. **Bake the Calzones**:
    - Carefully transfer the assembled calzones onto the prepared baking sheet.
    - Brush the tops of the calzones with olive oil and sprinkle with a little grated Parmesan cheese, if desired.
    - Bake in the preheated oven for 20-25 minutes, or until the calzones are golden brown and crispy.
5. **Finish and Serve**:
    - Remove the calzones from the oven and let them cool for a few minutes.
    - Slice each calzone in half and serve hot, optionally with extra marinara sauce on the side for dipping.

Tips:

- **Variations**: Feel free to customize the filling with your favorite ingredients such as different cheeses, vegetables, or meats.
- **Sealing**: Ensure the edges of the calzone are well-sealed to prevent filling from leaking during baking.
- **Serving**: Calzones are great for a meal on their own or served with a side salad for a complete meal.

Enjoy making and savoring this homemade Calzone with its flavorful filling and crispy crust—a perfect treat for pizza lovers!

Stromboli

Ingredients:

- 3 cups all-purpose flour
- 1 teaspoon salt
- 1 teaspoon sugar
- 1 packet (2 1/4 teaspoons) instant yeast
- 1 cup lukewarm water (about 110°F/45°C)
- 2 tablespoons olive oil

Instructions:

1. **Proof the Yeast**:
   - In a small bowl, combine the lukewarm water, sugar, and yeast. Let it sit for about 5-10 minutes, until foamy.
2. **Mix Dough**:
   - In a large mixing bowl or the bowl of a stand mixer fitted with a dough hook, combine the flour and salt.
   - Add the proofed yeast mixture and olive oil to the flour mixture. Mix until a dough starts to come together.
3. **Knead Dough**:
   - Knead the dough by hand on a lightly floured surface or with a stand mixer for about 5-7 minutes, until smooth and elastic. Add more flour if the dough is too sticky.
4. **First Rise**:
   - Place the dough in a lightly oiled bowl, turning once to coat. Cover with plastic wrap or a kitchen towel.
   - Let the dough rise in a warm place for about 1 hour, or until doubled in size.

Stromboli Filling:

Ingredients:

- 1 cup shredded mozzarella cheese
- 1/2 cup sliced pepperoni or cooked Italian sausage
- 1/2 cup thinly sliced ham or cooked chicken
- 1/4 cup sliced black olives
- 1/4 cup chopped roasted red peppers (from a jar)
- 1/4 cup grated Parmesan cheese
- 1/4 cup chopped fresh basil or parsley
- 1/2 cup marinara sauce, plus extra for serving
- Salt and pepper, to taste

Instructions:

1. **Prepare Filling**:
    - In a bowl, combine shredded mozzarella cheese, pepperoni or sausage, ham or chicken, black olives, roasted red peppers, Parmesan cheese, chopped basil or parsley, and marinara sauce. Season with salt and pepper to taste. Mix well.
2. **Assemble Stromboli**:
    - Preheat your oven to 400°F (200°C). Line a baking sheet with parchment paper.
    - Punch down the risen dough and roll it out on a lightly floured surface into a rectangle, about 12x16 inches.
3. **Fill and Roll**:
    - Spread the filling evenly over the dough, leaving a small border around the edges.
    - Starting from one long side, tightly roll up the dough jelly-roll style to encase the filling.
4. **Bake the Stromboli**:
    - Place the rolled Stromboli seam side down on the prepared baking sheet.
    - Brush the top with olive oil or melted butter for a golden crust.
    - Bake in the preheated oven for 25-30 minutes, or until the Stromboli is golden brown and crispy.
5. **Finish and Serve**:
    - Remove the Stromboli from the oven and let it cool for a few minutes.
    - Slice into thick slices and serve hot, optionally with extra marinara sauce for dipping.

Tips:

- **Variations**: Feel free to customize the filling with your favorite meats, cheeses, and vegetables.
- **Sealing**: Make sure to pinch the edges tightly when rolling up the Stromboli to prevent filling from leaking.
- **Serving**: Stromboli is great for a meal on its own or served with a side salad for a complete meal.

Enjoy making and enjoying this homemade Stromboli, filled with savory goodness and wrapped in a crispy crust—a perfect dish for pizza enthusiasts!

BBQ Pulled Pork Pizza

Ingredients:

- 1 lb pork shoulder or pork butt
- 1 cup BBQ sauce (homemade or store-bought)
- 1/2 cup chicken broth or water
- 1 tablespoon olive oil
- Salt and pepper, to taste

Instructions:

1. **Prepare the Pork**:
   - Season the pork shoulder with salt and pepper.
   - In a large skillet or Dutch oven, heat olive oil over medium-high heat. Brown the pork shoulder on all sides, about 3-4 minutes per side.
2. **Cook the Pork**:
   - Transfer the browned pork shoulder to a slow cooker. Pour BBQ sauce and chicken broth or water over the pork.
   - Cover and cook on low for 8 hours or on high for 4-5 hours, until the pork is tender and easily shreds with a fork.
3. **Shred the Pork**:
   - Remove the pork from the slow cooker and shred it using two forks. Discard any excess fat.
4. **Assemble BBQ Pulled Pork Pizza**:

Pizza Ingredients:

- Prepared pizza dough (homemade or store-bought)
- 1 cup BBQ sauce (homemade or store-bought)
- 2 cups shredded mozzarella cheese
- 1/2 red onion, thinly sliced
- 1/4 cup chopped fresh cilantro (optional)
- Olive oil, for drizzling

Instructions:

1. **Preheat Oven**:
   - Preheat your oven to the highest temperature setting (typically around 500°F/260°C). If using a pizza stone, place it in the oven during preheating.
2. **Roll Out Dough**:
   - On a lightly floured surface, roll out the pizza dough into a round or rectangular shape, about 1/4 inch thick.
3. **Prepare the Pizza**:
   - Transfer the rolled-out dough to a pizza peel or a parchment-lined baking sheet.

- Spread BBQ sauce evenly over the dough, leaving a small border around the edges.
 - Sprinkle shredded mozzarella cheese over the BBQ sauce.
 - Evenly distribute the shredded BBQ pulled pork and sliced red onion over the cheese.
4. **Bake the Pizza**:
 - If using a pizza stone, carefully slide the pizza onto the preheated stone in the oven. If using a baking sheet, place the baking sheet in the oven.
 - Bake for 10-12 minutes, or until the crust is golden brown and the cheese is bubbly and lightly browned.
5. **Finish and Serve**:
 - Remove the pizza from the oven and let it cool for a minute or two.
 - Optionally, sprinkle chopped fresh cilantro over the pizza.
 - Drizzle lightly with olive oil, slice, and serve hot.

Tips:

- **Pizza Dough**: Use your favorite homemade pizza dough recipe or store-bought dough for convenience.
- **BBQ Sauce**: Choose a BBQ sauce that you enjoy, whether it's sweet, smoky, or spicy.
- **Customization**: Feel free to add extra toppings like sliced jalapeños, bell peppers, or different cheeses to suit your taste.

Enjoy this BBQ Pulled Pork Pizza with its flavorful combination of BBQ sauce, tender pulled pork, melted cheese, and fresh toppings—a perfect treat for any pizza night!

Thai Chicken Pizza

Ingredients:

- 1 pre-made pizza dough (store-bought or homemade)
- 1 cup cooked and shredded chicken breast
- 1/2 cup Thai sweet chili sauce
- 1/2 cup shredded mozzarella cheese
- 1/2 cup shredded carrots
- 1/2 cup bean sprouts
- 1/4 cup chopped fresh cilantro
- 1/4 cup chopped green onions
- 1/4 cup chopped peanuts
- 2 tablespoons soy sauce
- 1 tablespoon sesame oil
- 1 tablespoon rice vinegar
- 1 teaspoon grated fresh ginger
- 1 garlic clove, minced
- Red pepper flakes (optional, for added spice)
- Olive oil (for brushing)

Instructions:

1. **Preheat Oven**: Preheat your oven to the temperature specified on your pizza dough package (usually around 425°F or 220°C).
2. **Prepare the Chicken**: In a bowl, mix the shredded chicken with soy sauce, sesame oil, rice vinegar, grated ginger, minced garlic, and red pepper flakes (if using). Set aside to marinate for about 10-15 minutes.
3. **Prepare the Sauce**: In another bowl, mix Thai sweet chili sauce with a tablespoon of soy sauce.
4. **Prepare the Pizza Dough**: Roll out the pizza dough on a lightly floured surface to your desired thickness. Place the rolled-out dough onto a pizza stone or a baking sheet.
5. **Assemble the Pizza**: Spread the Thai sweet chili sauce mixture evenly over the pizza dough. Sprinkle the shredded mozzarella cheese on top. Then, distribute the marinated chicken evenly over the cheese.
6. **Add Toppings**: Sprinkle shredded carrots, bean sprouts, chopped cilantro, and green onions evenly over the pizza.
7. **Bake the Pizza**: Place the pizza in the preheated oven and bake according to the pizza dough package instructions, typically about 12-15 minutes, or until the crust is golden brown and the cheese is melted and bubbly.
8. **Finish and Serve**: Once baked, remove the pizza from the oven and sprinkle chopped peanuts over the top. Slice the pizza and serve hot.

Tips:

- **Pizza Dough**: You can use store-bought pizza dough for convenience or make your own if preferred.
- **Spice Level**: Adjust the amount of red pepper flakes to your preference for spiciness.
- **Toppings**: Feel free to customize with additional toppings like bell peppers, onions, or pineapple to suit your taste.

Thai Chicken Pizza is a fantastic blend of savory, sweet, and spicy flavors that will surely impress your taste buds! Enjoy experimenting with different variations to find your perfect combination.

Teriyaki Chicken Pizza

Ingredients:

- 1 pre-made pizza dough (store-bought or homemade)
- 1 cup cooked and shredded chicken breast
- 1/2 cup teriyaki sauce (store-bought or homemade)
- 1 cup shredded mozzarella cheese
- 1/2 cup sliced red bell peppers
- 1/2 cup sliced green bell peppers
- 1/4 cup thinly sliced red onion
- 1/4 cup sliced mushrooms (optional)
- 1/4 cup chopped green onions
- 1/4 cup chopped fresh cilantro
- 1 tablespoon sesame seeds (optional)
- Olive oil (for brushing)

Instructions:

1. **Preheat Oven**: Preheat your oven to the temperature specified on your pizza dough package (usually around 425°F or 220°C).
2. **Prepare the Chicken**: In a bowl, mix the shredded chicken with 1/4 cup of teriyaki sauce. Set aside to marinate for about 10-15 minutes.
3. **Prepare the Pizza Dough**: Roll out the pizza dough on a lightly floured surface to your desired thickness. Place the rolled-out dough onto a pizza stone or a baking sheet.
4. **Assemble the Pizza**: Brush the rolled-out dough lightly with olive oil. Spread the remaining 1/4 cup of teriyaki sauce evenly over the pizza dough, leaving a small border around the edges for the crust. Sprinkle the shredded mozzarella cheese evenly over the sauce.
5. **Add Toppings**: Distribute the marinated teriyaki chicken evenly over the cheese. Scatter sliced red bell peppers, green bell peppers, red onion, and mushrooms (if using) over the pizza.
6. **Bake the Pizza**: Place the pizza in the preheated oven and bake according to the pizza dough package instructions, typically about 12-15 minutes, or until the crust is golden brown and the cheese is melted and bubbly.
7. **Finish and Serve**: Once baked, remove the pizza from the oven. Sprinkle chopped green onions, fresh cilantro, and sesame seeds (if using) over the hot pizza. Slice and serve immediately.

Tips:

- **Pizza Dough**: Use store-bought pizza dough or make your own dough.
- **Teriyaki Sauce**: You can use store-bought teriyaki sauce or make your own by combining soy sauce, mirin, sugar, garlic, and ginger.

- **Toppings**: Feel free to customize with additional vegetables or toppings like pineapple, cooked bacon, or even a drizzle of sriracha mayo for extra flavor.

Teriyaki Chicken Pizza offers a delightful blend of savory teriyaki flavors with the comforting appeal of pizza, making it a crowd-pleasing dish for any occasion. Enjoy experimenting with different toppings and variations to suit your taste!

Fig and Goat Cheese Pizza

Ingredients:

- 1 pre-made pizza dough (store-bought or homemade)
- 6-8 fresh figs, sliced
- 4 ounces goat cheese, crumbled
- 1 cup shredded mozzarella cheese
- 1/4 cup chopped walnuts
- 1/4 cup honey
- 1 tablespoon balsamic glaze (optional)
- Fresh arugula for topping (optional)
- Olive oil (for brushing)

Instructions:

1. **Preheat Oven:** Preheat your oven to the temperature specified on your pizza dough package (usually around 425°F or 220°C).
2. **Prepare the Pizza Dough:** Roll out the pizza dough on a lightly floured surface to your desired thickness. Place the rolled-out dough onto a pizza stone or a baking sheet.
3. **Assemble the Pizza:**
    - Brush the rolled-out dough lightly with olive oil.
    - Sprinkle the shredded mozzarella cheese evenly over the pizza dough.
    - Distribute the sliced figs and crumbled goat cheese over the cheese.
    - Sprinkle chopped walnuts evenly over the pizza.
4. **Bake the Pizza:** Place the pizza in the preheated oven and bake according to the pizza dough package instructions, typically about 12-15 minutes, or until the crust is golden brown and the cheese is melted and bubbly.
5. **Finish and Serve:**
    - Once baked, remove the pizza from the oven.
    - Drizzle honey over the hot pizza.
    - Optionally, drizzle balsamic glaze over the pizza for added flavor and presentation.
    - Top with fresh arugula for a peppery contrast (if using).
    - Slice and serve immediately.

Tips:

- **Pizza Dough:** Use store-bought pizza dough or make your own for a fresh taste.
- **Figs:** Use ripe figs for the best flavor. You can slice them thinly to distribute evenly over the pizza.
- **Goat Cheese:** Crumble the goat cheese evenly to ensure every bite has a bit of tangy goodness.

- **Honey and Balsamic Glaze:** These add a sweet and tangy finish to the pizza, enhancing the flavors of the figs and cheese.

This Fig and Goat Cheese Pizza is a wonderful blend of flavors that makes it perfect for a special occasion or a gourmet twist on homemade pizza night. Enjoy experimenting with the toppings and adjustments to suit your taste preferences!

Mushroom and Gorgonzola Pizza

Ingredients:

- 1 pre-made pizza dough (store-bought or homemade)
- 1 cup sliced mushrooms (such as cremini or button mushrooms)
- 1 cup crumbled Gorgonzola cheese
- 1 cup shredded mozzarella cheese
- 1/4 cup grated Parmesan cheese
- 1/4 cup chopped fresh parsley
- 1 tablespoon olive oil
- 1 garlic clove, minced
- Salt and pepper to taste
- Cornmeal (for dusting, optional)

Instructions:

1. **Preheat Oven:** Preheat your oven to the temperature specified on your pizza dough package (usually around 425°F or 220°C). If you have a pizza stone, place it in the oven while preheating.
2. **Prepare the Pizza Dough:**
    - If using a pizza stone, sprinkle it lightly with cornmeal. This helps prevent sticking and adds a nice texture to the crust.
    - Roll out the pizza dough on a lightly floured surface to your desired thickness. Transfer the rolled-out dough to the pizza stone or a baking sheet.
3. **Prepare the Mushrooms:**
    - In a skillet, heat olive oil over medium heat. Add minced garlic and sauté for about 30 seconds until fragrant.
    - Add sliced mushrooms to the skillet and sauté until they are tender and lightly browned, about 5-7 minutes. Season with salt and pepper to taste. Remove from heat and set aside.
4. **Assemble the Pizza:**
    - Brush the rolled-out dough lightly with olive oil.
    - Sprinkle shredded mozzarella cheese evenly over the pizza dough.
    - Distribute the sautéed mushrooms evenly over the cheese.
    - Crumble Gorgonzola cheese evenly over the mushrooms.
    - Sprinkle grated Parmesan cheese over the top.
5. **Bake the Pizza:**
    - Place the pizza in the preheated oven (on the pizza stone if using) and bake according to the pizza dough package instructions, typically about 12-15 minutes, or until the crust is golden brown and the cheese is melted and bubbly.
6. **Finish and Serve:**
    - Once baked, remove the pizza from the oven.
    - Sprinkle chopped fresh parsley over the hot pizza for a burst of freshness.

- Slice and serve immediately.

Tips:

- **Pizza Dough:** Use store-bought pizza dough or make your own for a personalized touch.
- **Cheese:** Gorgonzola provides a bold flavor, but you can adjust the amount to your taste preference. Blue cheese or even goat cheese can be substituted if desired.
- **Mushrooms:** Sautéing the mushrooms with garlic enhances their flavor. Ensure they are cooked until tender before adding them to the pizza.
- **Variations:** Add caramelized onions, spinach, or a drizzle of balsamic glaze for additional flavor layers.

This Mushroom and Gorgonzola Pizza is a savory treat that's perfect for any pizza night. Enjoy the rich flavors and customize it with your favorite toppings to make it your own!

Margherita with Burrata Pizza

Ingredients:

- 1 pre-made pizza dough (store-bought or homemade)
- 1/2 cup marinara sauce or pizza sauce
- 2-3 ripe tomatoes, thinly sliced
- 8 ounces burrata cheese
- Fresh basil leaves, torn or chopped
- 1 tablespoon olive oil
- Salt and pepper to taste
- Optional: Garlic cloves (for flavoring the crust)

Instructions:

1. **Preheat Oven:** Preheat your oven to the highest temperature possible, typically around 500°F (260°C). If you have a pizza stone, place it in the oven while preheating.
2. **Prepare the Pizza Dough:**
   - Roll out the pizza dough on a lightly floured surface to your desired thickness. If you like, rub a bit of olive oil on the crust and rub a cut garlic clove on the edges for added flavor.
3. **Assemble the Pizza:**
   - Spread marinara or pizza sauce evenly over the rolled-out pizza dough, leaving a small border for the crust.
   - Arrange the thinly sliced tomatoes evenly over the sauce.
   - Tear or chop the burrata cheese into pieces and distribute it evenly over the pizza.
   - Drizzle a tablespoon of olive oil over the pizza.
   - Season with salt and pepper to taste.
4. **Bake the Pizza:**
   - Transfer the assembled pizza onto the preheated pizza stone or a baking sheet.
   - Bake in the preheated oven for about 10-12 minutes, or until the crust is golden brown and the cheese is melted and bubbly.
5. **Finish and Serve:**
   - Remove the pizza from the oven.
   - Sprinkle torn or chopped fresh basil leaves over the hot pizza.
   - Optionally, drizzle a little more olive oil over the top for added richness.
   - Slice and serve immediately while the burrata is still warm and creamy.

Tips:

- **Pizza Dough:** Use store-bought pizza dough or make your own for a personalized touch.

- **Burrata Cheese:** Burrata is a creamy cheese with a soft center. It adds a luxurious texture to the pizza. You can substitute with fresh mozzarella if burrata is not available.
- **Tomatoes:** Use ripe tomatoes for the best flavor. If they release too much moisture, you can blot them with paper towels before placing them on the pizza.
- **Fresh Basil:** Adding fresh basil right after baking enhances the pizza's aroma and flavor

This Margherita with Burrata Pizza is a simple yet elegant dish that highlights fresh ingredients and creamy cheese. It's perfect for a cozy dinner or a gathering with friends. Enjoy the rich flavors and creamy texture of the burrata cheese with each bite!

Caramelized Onion and Brie Pizza

Ingredients:

- 1 pre-made pizza dough (store-bought or homemade)
- 2 large onions, thinly sliced
- 8 ounces Brie cheese, rind removed and sliced
- 1/4 cup grated Parmesan cheese
- 2 tablespoons olive oil
- 1 tablespoon balsamic vinegar
- 1 tablespoon brown sugar
- Fresh thyme leaves (optional)
- Salt and pepper to taste

Instructions:

1. **Preheat Oven:** Preheat your oven to the temperature specified on your pizza dough package (usually around 425°F or 220°C). If you have a pizza stone, place it in the oven while preheating.
2. **Caramelize the Onions:**
    - Heat 1 tablespoon of olive oil in a large skillet over medium heat.
    - Add thinly sliced onions and sauté until they start to soften, about 5 minutes.
    - Reduce the heat to medium-low and continue cooking, stirring occasionally, until the onions are golden brown and caramelized, about 20-25 minutes.
    - Stir in balsamic vinegar and brown sugar during the last few minutes of cooking. Season with salt and pepper to taste. Remove from heat and set aside.
3. **Prepare the Pizza Dough:**
    - Roll out the pizza dough on a lightly floured surface to your desired thickness. Transfer the rolled-out dough to a pizza stone or a baking sheet.
4. **Assemble the Pizza:**
    - Brush the rolled-out dough lightly with olive oil.
    - Spread the caramelized onions evenly over the pizza dough.
    - Arrange slices of Brie cheese evenly over the onions.
    - Sprinkle grated Parmesan cheese over the top.
    - Optionally, sprinkle fresh thyme leaves over the pizza for added flavor.
5. **Bake the Pizza:**
    - Place the pizza in the preheated oven (on the pizza stone if using) and bake according to the pizza dough package instructions, typically about 12-15 minutes, or until the crust is golden brown and the cheese is melted and bubbly.
6. **Finish and Serve:**
    - Remove the pizza from the oven.
    - Let it cool for a minute or two, then slice and serve hot.

Tips:

- **Pizza Dough:** Use store-bought pizza dough or make your own for a personalized touch.
- **Brie Cheese:** Removing the rind from the Brie helps it melt evenly over the pizza.
- **Caramelized Onions:** Take your time to properly caramelize the onions to bring out their natural sweetness.
- **Variations:** Add cooked bacon or prosciutto slices for a meaty twist, or top with arugula dressed with lemon juice and olive oil just before serving for a fresh contrast.

This Caramelized Onion and Brie Pizza is a delightful blend of sweet and savory flavors that's perfect for a cozy dinner at home or a special gathering with friends. Enjoy the creamy richness of the Brie and the sweetness of the caramelized onions in every bite!

Pear and Gorgonzola Pizza

Ingredients:

- 1 pre-made pizza dough (store-bought or homemade)
- 2 ripe pears, thinly sliced
- 4 ounces Gorgonzola cheese, crumbled
- 1 cup shredded mozzarella cheese
- 1/4 cup chopped walnuts or pecans
- 1/4 cup caramelized onions (optional, for extra sweetness)
- Fresh thyme leaves (optional)
- Olive oil (for brushing)
- Salt and pepper to taste

Instructions:

1. **Preheat Oven:** Preheat your oven to the temperature specified on your pizza dough package (typically around 425°F or 220°C). If you have a pizza stone, place it in the oven while preheating.
2. **Prepare the Pizza Dough:**
    - Roll out the pizza dough on a lightly floured surface to your desired thickness. Transfer the rolled-out dough to a pizza stone or a baking sheet.
3. **Assemble the Pizza:**
    - Brush the rolled-out dough lightly with olive oil.
    - Sprinkle shredded mozzarella cheese evenly over the pizza dough.
    - Arrange the thinly sliced pears evenly over the cheese.
    - Crumble Gorgonzola cheese over the pears.
    - If using, distribute caramelized onions over the pizza.
    - Sprinkle chopped walnuts or pecans evenly over the pizza.
    - Optionally, sprinkle fresh thyme leaves over the top for added flavor.
4. **Bake the Pizza:**
    - Place the pizza in the preheated oven (on the pizza stone if using) and bake according to the pizza dough package instructions, typically about 12-15 minutes, or until the crust is golden brown and the cheese is melted and bubbly.
5. **Finish and Serve:**
    - Remove the pizza from the oven.
    - Let it cool for a minute or two, then slice and serve hot.

Tips:

- **Pizza Dough:** Use store-bought pizza dough or make your own for a personalized touch.
- **Pears:** Use ripe but firm pears for the best texture on the pizza.

- **Gorgonzola Cheese:** Its tangy flavor pairs beautifully with the sweet pears. Adjust the amount based on your preference.
- **Walnuts or Pecans:** Toasting them slightly before adding to the pizza enhances their flavor and crunch.

This Pear and Gorgonzola Pizza is a unique and delicious option for pizza night, combining sweet and savory elements that will delight your taste buds. Enjoy experimenting with different toppings and variations to make it your own!

Chicken Tikka Masala Pizza

Ingredients:

- 1 pre-made pizza dough (store-bought or homemade)
- 1 cup cooked and shredded chicken tikka (leftover or freshly made)
- 1/2 cup tikka masala sauce (store-bought or homemade)
- 1 cup shredded mozzarella cheese
- 1/2 cup sliced red onions
- 1/2 cup diced bell peppers (any color)
- Fresh cilantro leaves, chopped
- 1 tablespoon olive oil
- Salt and pepper to taste
- Optional: Red chili flakes or chopped green chilies for added spice

Instructions:

1. **Preheat Oven:** Preheat your oven to the temperature specified on your pizza dough package (typically around 425°F or 220°C). If you have a pizza stone, place it in the oven while preheating.
2. **Prepare the Pizza Dough:**
   - Roll out the pizza dough on a lightly floured surface to your desired thickness. Transfer the rolled-out dough to a pizza stone or a baking sheet.
3. **Assemble the Pizza:**
   - Brush the rolled-out dough lightly with olive oil.
   - Spread tikka masala sauce evenly over the pizza dough, leaving a small border around the edges for the crust.
   - Sprinkle shredded mozzarella cheese evenly over the sauce.
   - Distribute shredded chicken tikka, sliced red onions, and diced bell peppers evenly over the cheese.
   - Season with salt and pepper to taste.
   - If desired, sprinkle red chili flakes or chopped green chilies for added spice.
4. **Bake the Pizza:**
   - Place the pizza in the preheated oven (on the pizza stone if using) and bake according to the pizza dough package instructions, typically about 12-15 minutes, or until the crust is golden brown and the cheese is melted and bubbly.
5. **Finish and Serve:**
   - Remove the pizza from the oven.
   - Sprinkle chopped fresh cilantro over the hot pizza.
   - Slice and serve immediately while hot.

Tips:

- **Pizza Dough:** Use store-bought pizza dough or make your own for a personalized touch.
- **Chicken Tikka:** You can use leftover chicken tikka or prepare it fresh for this recipe. It's typically marinated and grilled or baked with Indian spices.
- **Tikka Masala Sauce:** Use store-bought tikka masala sauce or make your own using a recipe that includes tomato, cream, and a blend of Indian spices.
- **Vegetarian Option:** Omit the chicken and add more vegetables or paneer (Indian cottage cheese) for a vegetarian version.
- **Spice Level:** Adjust the amount of chili flakes or green chilies to suit your preference for spiciness.

Enjoy the bold flavors of Chicken Tikka Masala Pizza, combining the best of Indian cuisine with the comforting appeal of pizza!

Tandoori Paneer Pizza

Ingredients:

- 1 pre-made pizza dough (store-bought or homemade)
- 200 grams paneer, cut into cubes
- 1/2 cup plain yogurt
- 1 tablespoon tandoori masala powder
- 1 teaspoon ground cumin
- 1 teaspoon ground coriander
- 1 teaspoon paprika
- 1/2 teaspoon turmeric powder
- 1/2 teaspoon garam masala
- 2 tablespoons lemon juice
- 2 cloves garlic, minced
- 1 tablespoon ginger paste or minced ginger
- Salt and pepper to taste
- 1/2 cup sliced red onions
- 1/2 cup sliced bell peppers (any color)
- 1 cup shredded mozzarella cheese
- Fresh cilantro leaves, chopped
- Olive oil (for brushing)
- Optional: Red chili flakes or chopped green chilies for added spice

Instructions:

1. **Marinate the Paneer:**
    - In a bowl, combine yogurt, tandoori masala powder, ground cumin, ground coriander, paprika, turmeric powder, garam masala, lemon juice, minced garlic, ginger paste, salt, and pepper. Mix well.
    - Add paneer cubes to the marinade and coat them evenly. Allow to marinate for at least 30 minutes, or preferably up to 2 hours in the refrigerator.
2. **Preheat Oven:** Preheat your oven to the temperature specified on your pizza dough package (usually around 425°F or 220°C). If you have a pizza stone, place it in the oven while preheating.
3. **Prepare the Pizza Dough:**
    - Roll out the pizza dough on a lightly floured surface to your desired thickness. Transfer the rolled-out dough to a pizza stone or a baking sheet.
4. **Assemble the Pizza:**
    - Brush the rolled-out dough lightly with olive oil.
    - Spread a thin layer of yogurt (from the marinade) evenly over the pizza dough.
    - Arrange marinated paneer cubes, sliced red onions, and sliced bell peppers evenly over the pizza.
    - Sprinkle shredded mozzarella cheese evenly over the toppings.

- If desired, sprinkle red chili flakes or chopped green chilies for added spice.
5. **Bake the Pizza:**
    - Place the pizza in the preheated oven (on the pizza stone if using) and bake according to the pizza dough package instructions, typically about 12-15 minutes, or until the crust is golden brown and the cheese is melted and bubbly.
6. **Finish and Serve:**
    - Remove the pizza from the oven.
    - Sprinkle chopped fresh cilantro over the hot pizza.
    - Slice and serve immediately while hot.

Tips:

- **Pizza Dough:** Use store-bought pizza dough or make your own for a personalized touch.
- **Paneer:** Paneer is an Indian cottage cheese that holds up well to baking. If you prefer a softer texture, you can skip marinating and use plain paneer cubes.
- **Tandoori Marinade:** Adjust the spices according to your preference for heat and flavor.
- **Vegetarian Option:** This pizza is naturally vegetarian and can be made vegan by using dairy-free yogurt and cheese alternatives.
- **Serve with:** Enjoy with a side of mint chutney or a cucumber raita for an authentic Indian meal experience.

This Tandoori Paneer Pizza is a delightful way to enjoy the bold flavors of tandoori spices combined with the comfort of pizza. It's perfect for a unique dinner or to impress guests with its vibrant colors and delicious taste!

Mediterranean Lamb Pizza

Ingredients:

- 1 pre-made pizza dough (store-bought or homemade)
- 1/2 lb ground lamb
- 1/2 cup crumbled feta cheese
- 1/2 cup sliced black olives
- 1/2 cup sliced red onion
- 1/2 cup diced tomatoes
- 1/4 cup chopped fresh parsley
- 1/4 cup chopped fresh mint
- 2 cloves garlic, minced
- 1 tablespoon olive oil
- 1 teaspoon dried oregano
- Salt and pepper to taste
- Optional: Red pepper flakes for heat
- Olive oil (for brushing)

Instructions:

1. **Preheat Oven:** Preheat your oven to the temperature specified on your pizza dough package (typically around 425°F or 220°C). If you have a pizza stone, place it in the oven while preheating.
2. **Prepare the Lamb:**
    - Heat olive oil in a skillet over medium heat. Add minced garlic and sauté for about 30 seconds until fragrant.
    - Add ground lamb to the skillet, breaking it apart with a spoon. Cook until browned and cooked through, about 5-7 minutes.
    - Season with dried oregano, salt, and pepper to taste. Remove from heat and set aside.
3. **Prepare the Pizza Dough:**
    - Roll out the pizza dough on a lightly floured surface to your desired thickness. Transfer the rolled-out dough to a pizza stone or a baking sheet.
4. **Assemble the Pizza:**
    - Brush the rolled-out dough lightly with olive oil.
    - Spread the cooked lamb evenly over the pizza dough.
    - Sprinkle crumbled feta cheese, sliced black olives, sliced red onion, and diced tomatoes evenly over the lamb.
    - If desired, sprinkle red pepper flakes over the toppings for added heat.
5. **Bake the Pizza:**
    - Place the pizza in the preheated oven (on the pizza stone if using) and bake according to the pizza dough package instructions, typically about 12-15 minutes, or until the crust is golden brown and the cheese is melted and bubbly.

6. **Finish and Serve:**
    - Remove the pizza from the oven.
    - Sprinkle chopped fresh parsley and mint over the hot pizza.
    - Slice and serve immediately while hot.

Tips:

- **Pizza Dough:** Use store-bought pizza dough or make your own for a personalized touch.
- **Lamb:** For extra flavor, you can marinate the ground lamb with Mediterranean spices like cumin, paprika, and cinnamon before cooking.
- **Feta Cheese:** Use crumbled feta cheese for its tangy flavor that complements the lamb.
- **Fresh Herbs:** Chopped fresh parsley and mint add a burst of freshness to the pizza.
- **Variations:** Add roasted red peppers, artichoke hearts, or a drizzle of tzatziki sauce before serving for additional Mediterranean flavors.

This Mediterranean Lamb Pizza is a hearty and flavorful dish that's perfect for a family dinner or entertaining guests. Enjoy the rich combination of lamb, feta cheese, and Mediterranean-inspired toppings on a crispy pizza crust!

Brussels Sprouts and Bacon Pizza

Ingredients:

- 1 pre-made pizza dough (store-bought or homemade)
- 1 cup shredded mozzarella cheese
- 1 cup shredded fontina cheese (or another melty cheese of your choice)
- 1 cup Brussels sprouts, trimmed and thinly sliced
- 4-6 slices of bacon, cooked and chopped
- 1/4 cup grated Parmesan cheese
- 1 tablespoon olive oil
- 2 cloves garlic, minced
- Salt and pepper to taste
- Red pepper flakes (optional, for a bit of heat)

Instructions:

1. **Preheat Oven:** Preheat your oven to the temperature specified on your pizza dough package (typically around 425°F or 220°C). If you have a pizza stone, place it in the oven while preheating.
2. **Prepare the Brussels Sprouts:**
    - Heat olive oil in a skillet over medium heat. Add minced garlic and sauté for about 30 seconds until fragrant.
    - Add thinly sliced Brussels sprouts to the skillet and sauté for 3-4 minutes, until slightly softened. Season with salt and pepper to taste. Remove from heat and set aside.
3. **Prepare the Pizza Dough:**
    - Roll out the pizza dough on a lightly floured surface to your desired thickness. Transfer the rolled-out dough to a pizza stone or a baking sheet.
4. **Assemble the Pizza:**
    - Brush the rolled-out dough lightly with olive oil.
    - Spread shredded mozzarella and fontina cheeses evenly over the pizza dough.
    - Distribute cooked Brussels sprouts and chopped bacon evenly over the cheese.
    - Sprinkle grated Parmesan cheese over the toppings.
    - If desired, sprinkle red pepper flakes over the pizza for added heat.
5. **Bake the Pizza:**
    - Place the pizza in the preheated oven (on the pizza stone if using) and bake according to the pizza dough package instructions, typically about 12-15 minutes, or until the crust is golden brown and the cheese is melted and bubbly.
6. **Finish and Serve:**
    - Remove the pizza from the oven.
    - Let it cool for a minute or two, then slice and serve hot.

Tips:

- **Pizza Dough:** Use store-bought pizza dough or make your own for a personalized touch.
- **Cheese:** Fontina cheese melts beautifully and adds a creamy texture, but you can substitute with another melty cheese like provolone or Gruyère.
- **Brussels Sprouts:** Slicing the Brussels sprouts thinly ensures they cook quickly and evenly on the pizza.
- **Bacon:** Use crispy bacon for added texture and flavor. You can also use pancetta or turkey bacon as alternatives.
- **Variations:** Add caramelized onions, pine nuts, or a drizzle of balsamic glaze for additional flavor layers.

This Brussels Sprouts and Bacon Pizza is a delightful combination of flavors and textures, perfect for a cozy dinner or casual gathering. Enjoy the hearty Brussels sprouts, smoky bacon, and gooey cheese on a crispy pizza crust!

Peking Duck Pizza

Ingredients:

- 1 pre-made pizza dough (store-bought or homemade)
- 1 cup shredded Peking duck meat (from a cooked Peking duck)
- 1/2 cup hoisin sauce
- 1 cup shredded mozzarella cheese
- 1/2 cup shredded Gruyère cheese (or substitute with another cheese like fontina)
- 1/2 cup thinly sliced cucumber
- 1/4 cup sliced scallions (green parts)
- 1 tablespoon sesame seeds
- 1 tablespoon chopped fresh cilantro (optional)
- Olive oil (for brushing)
- Salt and pepper to taste

Instructions:

1. **Preheat Oven:** Preheat your oven to the temperature specified on your pizza dough package (usually around 425°F or 220°C). If you have a pizza stone, place it in the oven while preheating.
2. **Prepare the Pizza Dough:**
   - Roll out the pizza dough on a lightly floured surface to your desired thickness. Transfer the rolled-out dough to a pizza stone or a baking sheet.
3. **Assemble the Pizza:**
   - Brush the rolled-out dough lightly with olive oil.
   - Spread hoisin sauce evenly over the pizza dough, leaving a small border for the crust.
   - Sprinkle shredded mozzarella cheese and Gruyère cheese evenly over the sauce.
   - Distribute shredded Peking duck meat evenly over the cheese.
   - Arrange thinly sliced cucumber over the pizza.
   - Season with salt and pepper to taste.
4. **Bake the Pizza:**
   - Place the pizza in the preheated oven (on the pizza stone if using) and bake according to the pizza dough package instructions, typically about 12-15 minutes, or until the crust is golden brown and the cheese is melted and bubbly.
5. **Finish and Serve:**
   - Remove the pizza from the oven.
   - Sprinkle sliced scallions, sesame seeds, and chopped fresh cilantro (if using) over the hot pizza.
   - Slice and serve immediately while hot.

Tips:

- **Pizza Dough:** Use store-bought pizza dough or make your own for a personalized touch.
- **Peking Duck Meat:** You can find Peking duck pre-cooked at some Asian markets or prepare it yourself using a Peking duck recipe.
- **Hoisin Sauce:** Adjust the amount of hoisin sauce to your taste preference.
- **Cucumber:** Thinly sliced cucumber adds a refreshing crunch to balance the rich flavors of the duck and cheese.
- **Garnish:** The sesame seeds, scallions, and cilantro add a touch of freshness and authenticity to the pizza.

Enjoy the unique and delicious flavors of Peking Duck Pizza, combining the best of Chinese cuisine with the beloved pizza format!

Ratatouille Pizza

Ingredients:

- 1 pre-made pizza dough (store-bought or homemade)
- 1 cup marinara sauce or pizza sauce
- 1 small eggplant, thinly sliced into rounds
- 1 small zucchini, thinly sliced into rounds
- 1 small yellow squash, thinly sliced into rounds
- 1 red bell pepper, thinly sliced
- 1 yellow bell pepper, thinly sliced
- 1 onion, thinly sliced
- 2-3 cloves garlic, minced
- 1 teaspoon dried thyme
- 1 teaspoon dried oregano
- Salt and pepper to taste
- 1 cup shredded mozzarella cheese
- 1/4 cup grated Parmesan cheese
- Olive oil (for brushing and sautéing)
- Fresh basil leaves, chopped (for garnish)

Instructions:

1. **Preheat Oven:** Preheat your oven to the temperature specified on your pizza dough package (typically around 425°F or 220°C). If you have a pizza stone, place it in the oven while preheating.
2. **Prepare the Vegetables:**
    - Heat a tablespoon of olive oil in a large skillet over medium-high heat.
    - Add minced garlic and sauté for about 30 seconds until fragrant.
    - Add sliced eggplant, zucchini, yellow squash, red bell pepper, yellow bell pepper, and onion to the skillet.
    - Season with dried thyme, dried oregano, salt, and pepper.
    - Sauté for 8-10 minutes, stirring occasionally, until the vegetables are softened and lightly browned. Remove from heat and set aside.
3. **Prepare the Pizza Dough:**
    - Roll out the pizza dough on a lightly floured surface to your desired thickness. Transfer the rolled-out dough to a pizza stone or a baking sheet.
4. **Assemble the Pizza:**
    - Brush the rolled-out dough lightly with olive oil.
    - Spread marinara or pizza sauce evenly over the pizza dough, leaving a small border for the crust.
    - Arrange the sautéed vegetables evenly over the sauce.
    - Sprinkle shredded mozzarella cheese and grated Parmesan cheese evenly over the vegetables.

5. **Bake the Pizza:**
    - Place the pizza in the preheated oven (on the pizza stone if using) and bake according to the pizza dough package instructions, typically about 12-15 minutes, or until the crust is golden brown and the cheese is melted and bubbly.
6. **Finish and Serve:**
    - Remove the pizza from the oven.
    - Sprinkle chopped fresh basil leaves over the hot pizza.
    - Slice and serve immediately while hot.

Tips:

- **Pizza Dough:** Use store-bought pizza dough or make your own for a personalized touch.
- **Vegetables:** Ratatouille traditionally includes eggplant, zucchini, peppers, and onions, but feel free to adjust the vegetables based on what you have or prefer.
- **Cheese:** Mozzarella and Parmesan cheeses complement the flavors of the vegetables well, but you can also use other cheeses like goat cheese or feta for variation.
- **Herbs:** Fresh basil adds a final touch of freshness, but you can also use other herbs like parsley or thyme.

This Ratatouille Pizza is a delicious and satisfying meal that celebrates the flavors of summer vegetables in a new and exciting way. Enjoy the colorful and wholesome goodness of ratatouille on a crispy pizza crust!

Blueberry Dessert Pizza

Ingredients:

- 1 pre-made pizza dough (store-bought or homemade)
- 8 oz cream cheese, softened
- 1/2 cup powdered sugar
- 1 teaspoon vanilla extract
- 1 cup fresh blueberries
- 1/4 cup sliced almonds (optional, for topping)
- 2 tablespoons honey or maple syrup, for drizzling

Instructions:

1. **Preheat Oven:** Preheat your oven to the temperature specified on your pizza dough package (typically around 425°F or 220°C). If you have a pizza stone, place it in the oven while preheating.
2. **Prepare the Pizza Dough:**
   - Roll out the pizza dough on a lightly floured surface to your desired thickness. Transfer the rolled-out dough to a pizza stone or a baking sheet.
3. **Bake the Pizza Dough:**
   - Bake the pizza dough in the preheated oven according to the package instructions, usually about 10-12 minutes or until the crust is golden brown. Remove from the oven and let it cool completely.
4. **Prepare the Cream Cheese Spread:**
   - In a mixing bowl, beat the softened cream cheese until smooth.
   - Add powdered sugar and vanilla extract. Mix until well combined and creamy.
5. **Assemble the Pizza:**
   - Once the pizza crust has cooled, spread the cream cheese mixture evenly over the crust, leaving a small border around the edges.
   - Scatter fresh blueberries evenly over the cream cheese layer.
   - If using, sprinkle sliced almonds over the blueberries.
6. **Drizzle with Honey or Maple Syrup:**
   - Drizzle honey or maple syrup over the top of the pizza for added sweetness.
7. **Slice and Serve:**
   - Slice the dessert pizza into wedges or squares.
   - Serve immediately and enjoy the sweet and tangy flavors of the blueberries and creamy cream cheese on the crispy pizza crust!

Tips:

- **Pizza Dough:** Use a basic pizza dough that bakes up crisp and sturdy to hold the toppings.

- **Cream Cheese:** Make sure the cream cheese is softened to room temperature for easy spreading.
- **Blueberries:** Fresh blueberries work best for this dessert pizza, but you can also use frozen blueberries that have been thawed and drained.
- **Variations:** Feel free to customize your dessert pizza with other fruits such as strawberries, raspberries, or even a mix of berries.

This Blueberry Dessert Pizza is perfect for a sweet ending to any meal or as a special treat for gatherings. It's easy to prepare and sure to impress with its vibrant colors and delicious flavors!